ENVIRONMENTAL STUDIES

LOOKING AROUND

Manisha Malhotra

ARIHANT PRAKASHAN, MEERUT

WORKBOOK Environmental Studies 4th

Published by Arihant Prakashan, Meerut

ॐ **Administrative & Production Offices**

Regd. Office
'Ramchhaya' 4577/15, Agarwal Road, Darya Ganj, New Delhi -110002
Tele: 011- 47630600, 43518550; Fax: 011- 23280316

Head Office
Kalindi, TP Nagar, Meerut (UP) - 250002
Tel: 0121-2401479, 2512970, 4004199; Fax: 0121-2401648

ॐ **Sales & Support Offices**

Agra, Ahmedabad, Bengaluru, Bhubaneswar, Bareilly, Chennai, Delhi, Guwahati, Hyderabad, Jaipur, Jhansi, Kolkata, Lucknow, Meerut, Nagpur & Pune.

ॐ **ISBN** 978-93-11122-01-4

ॐ **Price** ₹ 80.00

Production Team

Publishing Manager
Keshav Mohan, Amit Verma

Project Head
Karishma Yadav

Project Coordinator
Divya Gusain

Project Editor
Gajendra Singh

Cover Designer
Shanu Mansoori

Inner Designer
Ravi Negi

DTP Operator
Vinay Sharma

Proof Readers
Garima Sharma, Pooja Saini

For further information about the books published by Arihant, log on to www.arihantbooks.com or e-mail at info@arihantbooks.com

Workbook, Why?

"Knowledge will not be with you for Long Unless You Practice"

This quotation answer the above question 'Workbook, Why ?'
perfectly, i.e., Workbooks are made to give the students practice required to achieve
perfection and mastery in the subject. These are the only Workbooks, which are strictly
based on **NCERT, the only recommended books by Govt. of India & CBSE**
(reference Circular No. Acad-41/2015 dated 20th July 2015).

Given below is the detailed description of Workbook and some of its special features

ONLY WORKBOOK BASED ON NCERT

NCERT textbooks are the only textbooks, which have been prepared according to
National Curriculum Framework, which discourages the idea of rote learning rather
they focus on understanding and try to make the students able to identify the way of
problem solving.

Keeping the importance of NCERT textbooks in mind we have prepared this Workbook,
strictly based on NCERT content. This Workbook will complement NCERT by providing
practice on the material given in each chapter of NCERT textbook, making the students
understand the chapter completely.

WORKBOOK- PURPOSE, USE & FEATURES

This Workbook, through its **numerous exercises** having different **variety of
questions** covering each and every fact of NCERT, will prove to be **equally useful** for
both, **Classroom** and **at Home**. One more purpose of this Workbook is to provide the
students a **systematic practice** of the content taught in the class and what they study
in the textbooks.

Some special features of this Workbook are

- Complete Coverage of each chapter for complete practice

- Different variety of questions; Fill in the Blanks, True-False, Matching, Multiple
  Choice Questions, Differentiate Between, Define the Following, Very Short
  Answer, Short Answer, Long Answer Type, etc.

- Many questions given in each chapter are related with day-to-day activities
  making them interesting to solve.

- Keeps the students actively engaged with the content and develop enquiry
  skills.

WORKBOOK-DESIGNED TO IMPROVE SUBJECT ABILITIES

All the material given in this Workbook is tailored to suit subject content with equal
support on learning, which will surely help students to boost their abilities and
confidence in the subject.

*I look forward for the feedback from students, teachers and parents for the further improvement of
the contents of this book. I will try to update the contents according to your feedback in further
editions of this Workbook.*

The Publisher

Contents

Chapter 1	Going to School	1-4
Chapter 2	Ear to Ear	5-8
Chapter 3	A Day with Nandu	9-12
Chapter 4	The Story of Amrita	13-16
Chapter 5	Anita and the Honeybees	17-20
Chapter 6	Omana's Journey	21-24
Chapter 7	From the Window	25-28
Chapter 8	Reaching Grandmother's House	29-32
Chapter 9	Changing Families	33-35
Chapter 10	Hu Tu Tu, Hu Tu Tu	36-38
Chapter 11	The Valley of Flowers	39-41
Chapter 12	Changing Times	42-45
Chapter 13	A River's Tale	46-48
Chapter 14	Basva's Farm	49-52
Chapter 15	From Market to Home	53-56
Chapter 16	A Busy Month	57-60
Chapter 17	Nandita in Mumbai	61-64
Chapter 18	Too Much Water, Too Little Water	65-68
Chapter 19	Abdul in the Garden	69-72
Chapter 20	Eating Together	73-76
Chapter 21	Food and Fun	77-79
Chapter 22	The World in my Home	80-83
Chapter 23	Pochampalli	84-87
Chapter 24	Home and Abroad	88-91
Chapter 25	Spicy Riddles	92-95
Chapter 26	Defence Officer : Wahida	96-99
Chapter 27	Chuskit Goes to School	100-103
● Answers		104-108

Chapter 1

Going to School

1. Select the best option.

(i) Which of the following work cannot be done by a pulley?

(a) Helping a trolley move across a river.

(b) Helping a blind man cross the road.

(c) Taking out water from a well.

(d) Lifting bricks to a height.

(ii) You can reach school on a bullock-cart, if you have to

(a) cross a thick forest.　　(b) go over rocky footpaths.

(c) move through snow.　　(d) move through green fields.

(iii) The *jugad* is made out of

(a) a motorcycle.　　(b) planks of wood.

(c) waste material.　　(d) All of these.

(iv) Knee-high water is found after rain in

(a) Assam.　　(b) Uttarakhand.

(c) Dense forest.　　(d) Ladakh.

(v) The transport used for going to school in ___________ makes a *phut-phut-phut* sound.

(a) Uttarakhand　　(b) Kerala

(c) Gujarat　　(d) Northern hills

2. Write 'T' for True and 'F' for False statements.

(i) We can ride a bicycle to go to school, if it can be reached by road.

(ii) We can go to school on a trolley if the school lies across a river.

(iii) We can ride a *jugad* to reach school if it lies across green fields.

(iv) We cannot reach school, if we have to cross a road bridge.

(v) We can ride a camel-cart to school through a thick forest.

3. Fill in the blanks.

(i) A *vallam* is used to reach school in some parts of ____________ .

(ii) In parts of Assam, children reach school by crossing over ____________ bridges.

(iii) Children in the mountains of Uttarakhand reach school by going on ____________ .

(iv) In Rajasthan, children use a ____________ to reach school.

(v) ____________ does not pass through thick jungle.

4. Match the type of bridge in Column A with the material it is made of in Column B by drawing arrows.

Column A		Column B	
(i)	Trolley bridge	(a)	Bricks, iron rods and cement
(ii)	Bamboo bridge	(b)	Wood and iron rope
(iii)	Cement bridge	(c)	Iron
(iv)	Iron bridge	(d)	Bamboo and rope

Very Short Answer Type Questions

5. Answer in one word or one sentence.

(i) Where is a camel-cart used for going to school?

(ii) By which ride the children can travel through the difficult roads by their own?

(iii) When we go to school through a jungle, what sounds can we hear?

(iv) If we have to reach school by going through snow, what happens if the snow is soft?

(v) Who will face difficulty to walk on rocky path?

(vi) Which type of bridge may have steps?

6. The names of some forms of transport are given below in jumbled form (in some, both words are jumbled). Write the correct name of the form of transport against each.

  (i) eilccyb   _______________________

 (ii) eamlc tarc   _______________________

(iii) eolrtyl   _______________________

(iv) obambo reigbd   _______________________

 (v) aamllv   _______________________

7. (i) Which methods for going to school

    (a) require the least effort?

    (b) are the most dangerous?

    (c) require some skill or practice?

    (d) are the fastest?

    (e) involve going on roads?

 (ii) In which mode of transportation

    (a) use animals?

    (b) require the children to walk?

    (c) require motorised or other type of transportation mechanism?

    (d) require the children to use their own energy other than walking?

Short Answer Type Question

8. Answer in 30 – 40 words.

  (i) What is a trolley? How it moves?

  (ii) How 'Jugad' is made?

  (iii) Compare the difficulties between going to school as shown in Picture 1 and Picture 2.

Picture 1

Picture 2

Long Answer Type Question

9. What are the differences between a bamboo bridge and cement bridge?

Think, Find and Write

10. School children face many problems while travelling to school. Mention any five such problems.

[Chapter **2**]

Ear to Ear

1. Select the best option.

   (i) Which of the following animals has tiny holes on both sides of the head to hear?

      (a) Giraffe   ☐   (b) Crow   ☐

      (c) Tiger   ☐   (d) Donkey   ☐

   (ii) The __________ has ears like fans.

      (a) elephant   ☐   (b) monkey   ☐

      (c) whale   ☐   (d) hen   ☐

  (iii) The donkey has ears

      (a) which cannot be seen.   ☐   (b) on the top of its head.   ☐

      (c) on the sides of its head.   ☐   (d) Both (a) and (c).   ☐

  (iv) The patterns by which animals may be recognised are due to

      (a) colour of their skin.   ☐   (b) hair on their skin.   ☐

      (c) feel of their skin.   ☐   (d) Both (a) and (c).   ☐

   (v) Now where do we see dinosaurs?

      (a) Only in forests   ☐   (b) Only in the zoo   ☐

      (c) In films and pictures   ☐   (d) None of these   ☐

2. Write 'T' for True and 'F' for False statements.

   (i) Our national animal is peacock.   ☐

   (ii) A fish has ears but we cannot see it.   ☐

  (iii) Buffaloes and cows have hair on their bodies.   ☐

  (iv) Sheep do not have hair on their bodies.   ☐

   (v) Squirrel lays eggs.   ☐

3. Fill in the blanks.

   (i) Usually we cannot see the holes used for hearing by a bird because they are covered by ____________ .

  (ii) If an animal does not have outer hair, it will not have any ____________ on its skin.

 (iii) Crocodiles and lizards hear by ____________ on the sides of their heads.

  (iv) All animals that give birth to their young ones have ____________ ears.

   (v) Animals not having visible ears can be recognised by having ____________ on their body.

4. Match the type of pattern in Column A with the animal in Column B by drawing arrows.

Column A		Column B	
(i)	Black stripes on white skin	(a)	Deer
(ii)	Black stripes on yellow-brown skin	(b)	Leopard
(iii)	Black spots on yellow-brown skin	(c)	Tiger
(iv)	White spots on yellow-brown skin	(d)	Zebra

5. Let us observe the pictures given below.

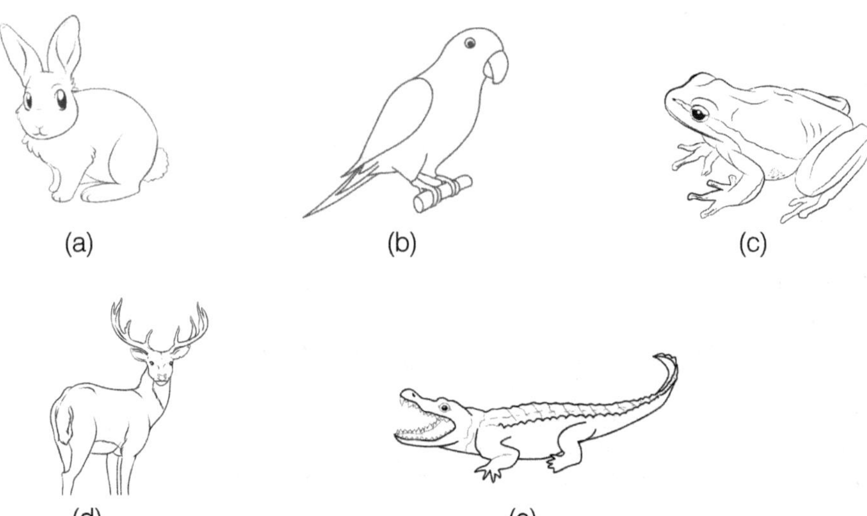

(a) (b) (c)

(d) (e)

Name the picture and tell which have visible ears by ticking Yes or No.

   (a) ______________________________   Yes/No

   (b) ______________________________   Yes/No

   (c) ______________________________   Yes/No

   (d) ______________________________   Yes/No

   (e) ______________________________   Yes/No

Very Short Answer Type Questions

6. Answer in one word or one sentence.

    (i) Name two animals which give birth to babies?

    (ii) Name any two animals which have ears on the sides of their head.

    (iii) How does a snake hear?

    (iv) Why do animals have different patterns on their bodies?

7. Answer the following questions based on the picture given below.

    (i) Which big animal is seen in the picture?

    (ii) What are the small animals doing?

Short Answer Type Questions

8. Answer in 30 – 40 words.

    (i) What is the reason that animals can be recognised by their skin?

(ii) How do birds hear?

9. Animals not having ears can still hear. How?

Long Answer Type Question

10. Explain the similarities and differences between a bird and cow regarding their bodies. How do they give birth to their babies?

Think, Find and Write

11. The names of some animals are given in jumbled form in the table given below. Complete the table.

Jumbled Name	Name of Animal	Has hair on skin / Does not have hair on skin	Lays eggs / Gives birth to young	Ears visible / not visible
HSFI				
TAPHNLEE				
KUCD				
PWORSAR				
EONYDK				
DARLPEO				
OFALFBU				
OEGNPI				

Chapter 3

A Day with Nandu

1. Select the best option.

(i) Elephants sleep for ____________ day.

(a) most of the ☐ (b) 4 to 6 hours in a ☐

(c) 12 to 16 hours in a ☐ (d) 2 to 4 hours in a ☐

(ii) A normal 3-month old baby elephant may weigh about

(a) 10 kg. ☐ (b) 50 kg. ☐

(c) 200 kg. ☐ (d) None of these ☐

(iii) Who complains that they have to dance on an empty stomach?

(a) The monkeys ☐ (b) The bears ☐

(c) Nandu ☐ (d) The horses ☐

(iv) Elephants move around in groups called

(a) colonies. ☐ (b) herds. ☐

(c) swarms. ☐ (d) None of these ☐

(v) Adult elephants eat

(a) meat and eggs. ☐ (b) sugar and grain. ☐

(c) forest fruits. ☐ (d) twigs and leaves. ☐

2. Write 'T' for True and 'F' for False statements.

(i) People specially call pigeons to feed them with grain. ☐

(ii) Children don't like cats. ☐

(iii) When horseshoe are fixed to a horse's hooves, the horse loves it. ☐

(iv) The oldest male is the leader of a herd of elephants. ☐

(v) Elephants lie in the mud to cool their bodies. ☐

3. Fill in the blanks.

(i) Male elephants stay in the herd till they are _____________ .

(ii) The grey forest that Nandu imagined he was in, was actually _____________ of his family members.

(iii) Living only in a basket the snake has forgotten what it is like in the _____________ and fresh air.

(iv) For entertainment, humans use three animals: _____________, _____________ and snakes.

(v) When baby elephants play, they pull each other's _____________.

4. Match the name in Column A with the activity in Column B by drawing arrows.

Column A		Column B	
(i)	Nandu	(a)	Follows *Nani Ma*
(ii)	*Amma*	(b)	Squirt water on Nandu
(iii)	*Nani Ma*	(c)	Drinks his mother's milk
(iv)	Nandu's cousins	(d)	Leads the herd

5. Match the pictures in Column A with the activities in Column B by drawing lines.

Column A	Column B	
(i)	(a)	Elephants playing
(ii)	(b)	Elephants cooling themselves
(iii)	(c)	Elephants feeding themselves
(iv)	(d)	Elephants drinking water

Very Short Answer Type Questions

6. Answer in one word or one sentence.

   (i) Why does a herd of elephants spread out in a forest?

   (ii) What sound does an elephant make?

   (iii) Is Nandu a male or female elephant?

7. Why is it important for elephants to live in herds?

Short Answer Type Questions

8. Answer in 30 – 40 words.

   (i) Why is the cat happier than the horse, the bear, or the monkey?

   (ii) Elephants use two methods to keep their bodies cool. Describe these methods in one sentence each.

9. Some animals have expressed their ill-treatment by humans in this chapter.
State this ill-treatment in one sentence for each of the four animals given in the chapter.

   (i)

   (ii)

   (iii)

   (iv)

Long Answer Type Question

10. Answer in 80 – 100 words.

(i) Nandu was a shy baby, but finally he played in the water with his cousins. Describe how this took place.

(ii) Briefly describe Nandu's day, listing his activities at the different times given below.

(a) Just after he woke up.

(b) After *Nani Ma* trumpetted.

(c) After the elephants had eaten.

(d) Just before sunset.

(e) What he did just before falling asleep?

Think, Find and Write

11. How are elephants useful to man?

12. Match the names of animals in Column A with the names of their groups in Column B by drawing arrows.

Column A	Column B
(i) Ducks	(a) Herd
(ii) Bees	(b) Flight
(iii) Elephants	(c) Pack
(iv) Pigeons	(d) Flock
(v) Fishes	(e) Caravan
(vi) Wolves	(f) Shoal
(vii) Camels	(g) Swarm

Chapter 4

The Story of Amrita

1. Select the best option.

(i) ___________ were Amrita's best friends.

    (a) Peacocks   ☐   (b) Animals   ☐

    (c) Schoolchildren   ☐   (d) Trees   ☐

(ii) Children of *Khejadli* played

    (a) hop skotch and gulli-danda.   ☐   (b) inside their homes.   ☐

    (c) in the shade of the trees.   ☐   (d) in the village playground.   ☐

(iii) The King wanted the trees to be cut because

    (a) the wood was needed for his palace.   ☐

    (b) they were very old.   ☐

    (c) all their leaves had fallen.   ☐

    (d) the villagers were his enemies.   ☐

(iv) The villagers protected the trees from being cut by

    (a) snatching away the woodcutters' axes.   ☐

    (b) requesting the King.   ☐

    (c) hugging the trees.   ☐

    (d) killing the woodcutters.   ☐

(v) The most common tree that grew in Amrita's village was the ___________ tree.

    (a) Neem   ☐   (b) *Khejadi*   ☐

    (c) Peepal   ☐   (d) None of these   ☐

2. Write 'T' for True and 'F' for False statements.

  (i) Amrita and her companions sacrificed their lives almost three hundred years ago.

 (ii) The elders of *Khejadli* village said that plants and animals can live without humans.

(iii) The King stopped the tree cutting when he came to know of the strong feelings of the villagers.

(iv) Today *Khejadli* village is again like a desert.

 (v) Leaves of the Khejadi tree are eaten by animals.

(vi) The story of Amrita is a true story.

3. Fill in the blanks.

  (i) The Bishnoi people, even today, protect ____________ .

 (ii) The King learnt about the villagers' respect for ___________ when he visited the village.

(iii) If we visit *Khejadli* village today we will find that the animals there ___________ without fear.

(iv) Amrita during her childhood wanted the trees to give ___________ to her.

 (v) The ___________ near Lalita's school wall has not been planted by anyone.

(vi) *Khejadli* village is located near ___________ in Rajasthan.

4. Given below are some pictures associated with Amrita and the story of *Khejadli* village. Write the number of each picture against the correct information associated with it.

Picture 1   Picture 2   Picture 3

Picture 4   Picture 5

Sentences

   (i) Amrita playing during her childhood.

  (ii) Amrita killed by the woodcutters.

 (iii) Amrita protects a tree from being cut.

 (iv) The village elders talking to the King.

  (v) The King asks the woodcutters to bring wood.

Very Short Answer Type Question

5. Answer in one word or one sentence.

   (i) Who are the Bishnois?

  (ii) When Amrita grew up, why did strangers visit her village?

 (iii) When Amrita hugged a tree, what did the woodcutters do before killing her?

 (iv) What did the King not believe?

  (v) In which areas is the *Khejadi* tree usually found?

Short Answer Type Question

6. Answer in 30 – 40 words.

   (i) How did the day of little Amrita usually begin?

  (ii) List two reasons due to which the *Khejadi* tree can survive in very poor conditions.

(iii) How was the village finally protected against cutting of trees?

(iv) Why did the king's men kill the villagers of *Khejadli*?

Long Answer Type Question

7. Answer in 80 – 100 words.

(i) How can we say that the King was not cruel? What orders did he give upon knowing of the villagers' deaths?

(ii) Describe the various use of the *Khejadi* tree.

Think, Find and Write

8. Mention three ways in which we can protect our trees from being cut without affecting our everyday life.

Chapter 5

Anita and the Honeybees

1. Select the best option.

(i) ______________ are the most important bees for the hive.

(a) Queen bees ☐   (b) Worker bees ☐

(c) Male bees ☐   (d) All of these ☐

(ii) Honeybees suck ____________ from the flowers.

(a) water ☐   (b) sugar ☐

(c) honey ☐   (d) nectar ☐

(iii) ____________ live and work like honeybees.

(a) Termites ☐   (b) Wasps ☐

(c) Ants ☐   (d) All of these ☐

(iv) Litchi trees give flowers in the month of

(a October. ☐   (b) December. ☐

(c) February. ☐   (d) April. ☐

(v) How does Anita now go to college?

(a) By a cycle ☐   (b) By a motorcycle ☐

(c) By train ☐   (d) Walking ☐

2. Write 'T' for True and 'F' for False statements.

(i) In childhood, Anita used to graze her cows. ☐

(ii) Anita studied only upto Class Vth. ☐

(iii) Anita was popular among the children she was teaching. ☐

(iv) At village meetings, Anita talks about the importance of bee-keeping. ☐

(v) Anita stays in Muzzafarpur district of Bihar. ☐

3. Fill in the blanks.

  (i) We need to do a ____________ course to keep bees.

 (ii) Honeybees lay their eggs from ____________ to ____________ .

(iii) The ____________ lays eggs.

(iv) Honeybees are kept in a ____________ .

 (v) There is ____________ Queen bee in a hive.

(vi) ____________ and ____________ are required to keep the bees.

4. Match the pictures in Column A with their descriptions in Column B by drawing lines.

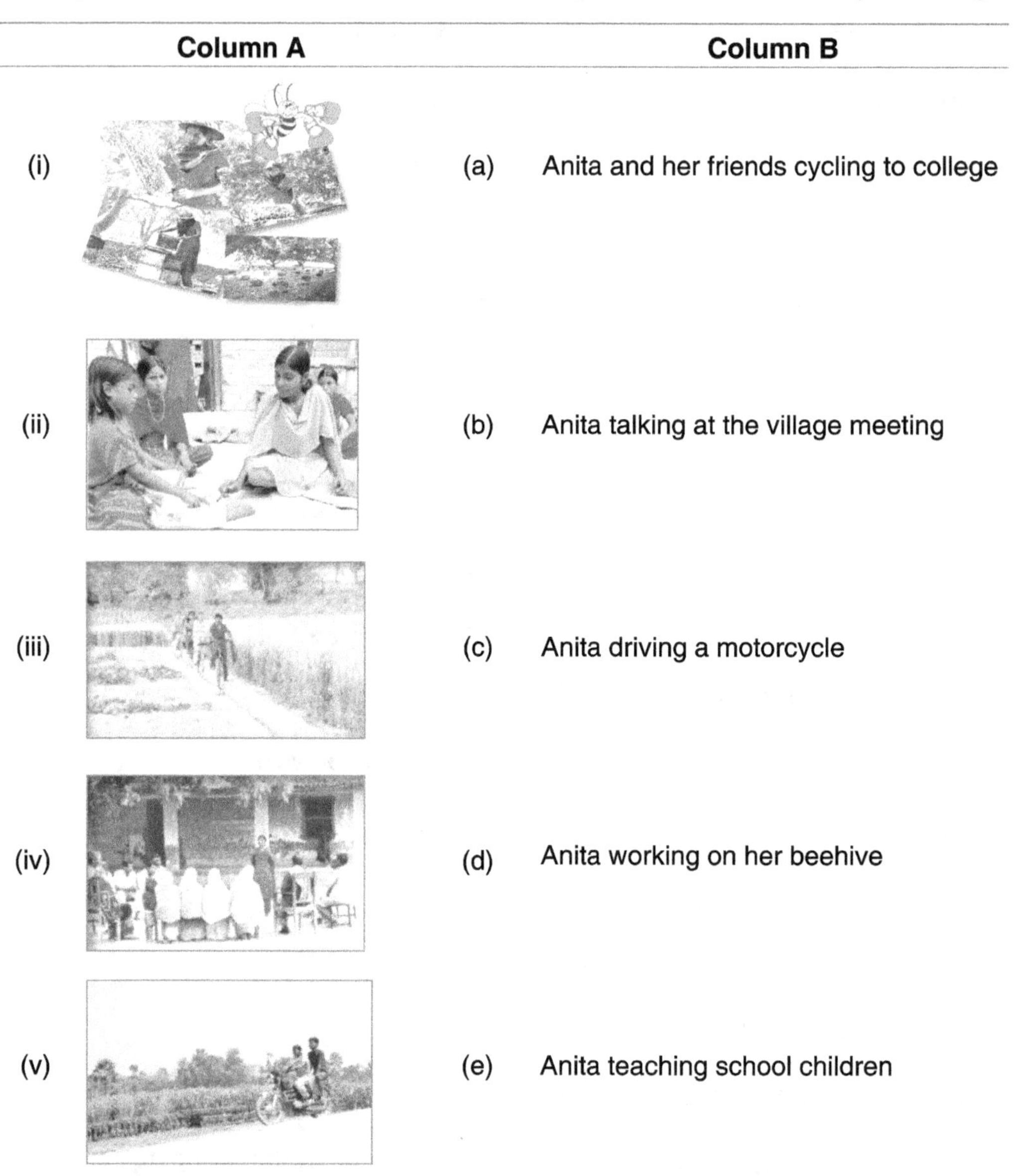

Column A	Column B
(i)	(a) Anita and her friends cycling to college
(ii)	(b) Anita talking at the village meeting
(iii)	(c) Anita driving a motorcycle
(iv)	(d) Anita working on her beehive
(v)	(e) Anita teaching school children

5. Given below are some sentences from the chapter. Put them in the correct sequence by numbering them from 1 to 8.

Number in Sequence

   (i) I want to become a wholesaler and get the right price of honey. _______

  (ii) I bought two boxes for keeping bees. _______

 (iii) Now I have 20 boxes. _______

 (iv) Many times the bee would sting me. _______

  (v) I got 12 kg of honey from each box. _______

 (vi) I joined the course in bee keeping. _______

 (vii) I bought sugar to make the syrup for honeybees. _______

(viii) I collected ₹ 5000 by teaching children. _______

Very Short Answer Type Question

6. Answer in one word or one sentence.

   (i) Why did Anita not go to school in the early part of her life?

  (ii) How did Anita manage to find money to start her bee-keeping activity?

 (iii) Who helped Anita when she wanted to get more time to study?

 (iv) What does Anita tell other villagers at the village meetings?

  (v) Why does Anita want to become a wholesaler of honey?

Short Answer Type Questions

7. Answer in 30 – 40 words.

    (i) Why did Anita's parents finally allow her to go to school?

    (ii) When Anita is attending her college, how is the bee-keeping work continued?

8. What did Anita do after collecting ₹ 5000?

Long Answer Type Question

9. Answer in 80 – 100 words.

    (i) Describe the duties of the different kinds of bees in the beehive.

    (ii) Describe how do the worker bees collect nectar from flowers.

Think, Find and Write

10. If a honeybee stings a person, what should be the first-aid given?

11. What are the various uses of honey which we get from honeybees?

Chapter 6

Omana's Journey

1. Select the best option.

(i) The doctor said that Radha shouldn't move her leg for

(a) six days.

(b) six months.

(c) six weeks.

(d) None of these

(ii) Omana passed her time on the train by

(a) writing her diary.

(b) looking out of the window.

(c) eating meals and snacks.

(d) All of these

(iii) Omana's train had started from

(a) Kozhikode.

(b) Valsad.

(c) Gandhidham.

(d) Not mentioned in her diary.

(iv) Radha did not go with Omana on the journey because

(a) Radha's *Amma* was ill.

(b) Radha's leg was fractured.

(c) Omana did not want her to go.

(d) None of these.

(v) At Valsad, Omana's family bought ___________ to eat.

(a) lemon rice

(b) *dhokla* with *chutney*

(c) *batata vada*

(d) bananas and *chikoos*

2. Write 'T' for True and 'F' for False statements.

(i) The train reached Valsad early in the morning.

(ii) Sunil and Ann were also going to Kerala.

(iii) Omana's *Amma* and *Appa* had got the middle berths in the compartment.

(iv) Omana's family checked their names on the reservation chart.

(v) The fields outside the window of the train were green with lots of trees.

3. Fill in the blanks.

    (i) _____________ and __________ were best friends.

    (ii) Radha fell down from ___________ and fractured her __________ leg.

    (iii) _____________ had the upper berths in their compartment.

    (iv) The sky becomes __________ in colour when the sun was __________ .

    (v) Sunil and Ann were going to their __________ house.

4. Given below are some happenings in Omana's journey. Put them in the correct sequence by numbering them from 1 to 8.

Number in Sequence

    (i) "Omana, write down everything about her trip in a diary." ___________

    (ii) Looking out of the window, I saw brown and dry fields. ___________

    (iii) The ticket collector came and checked their tickets. ___________

    (iv) We have just passed a station called Valsad. ___________

    (v) Omana's father booked the train tickets for both families. ___________

    (vi) There was no water in the bathroom. ___________

    (vii) Omana's family checked their names on the reservation chart. ___________

    (viii) *Amma* has opened the tiffin box. ___________

5. The names of some people in the railways are given below in jumbled form. Write their correct names.

    (i) AEETNRORVI RLKEC _______________

    (ii) CEIKTT OOCCLLRTE _______________

    (iii) NNEEGI REIRVD _______________

    (iv) EPRROT _______________

    (v) ADGRU _______________

6. Match the pictures in Column A with the description of what is happening in Column B by drawing lines.

Column A	Column B
(i)	(a) Train standing at station
(ii)	(b) Looking out of a compartment window
(iii)	(c) Ticket collector checking tickets

Very Short Answer Type Question

7. Answer in one word or one sentence.

(i) What did Sunil give Omana before going to sleep?

(ii) What food items were available at Valsad station?

(iii) Whose idea was it for Omana to write a diary of her journey?

(iv) What had Omana's *Amma* brought in the tiffin?

(v) Why couldn't Radha go with Omana to Kerala?

(vi) What is the job of the ticket collector?

Short Answer Type Question

8. Answer in 30 – 40 words.

(i) Omana has mentioned some people who were travelling with her family in their compartment. Describe them.

(ii) Why was it so crowded at the door of the coach when Omana's family were getting in?

(iii) Why didn't Omana brush her teeth at night? When would she be able to do so?

Long Answer Type Question

9. Answer in 80 – 100 words.

Describe what Omana saw outside the compartment from window after lunch.

Think, Find and Write

10. What food and clothes will you carry, if you will travel by a train?

11. How should we prepare for a long train journey like the one Omana took? Describe by taking example from the chapter.

Chapter 7

From the Window

1. Select the best option.

(i) Madgaon is in which state?

(a) Gujarat   (b) Maharashtra

(c) Kerala   (d) None of these

(ii) Which of the following vehicles run on diesel or petrol?

(a) Cars   (b) Trucks

(c) Autorickshaws   (d) All of these

(iii) During lunch Omana ate

(a) bananas and *idli-vada*.   (b) tea and *idli-vada*.

(c) coffee and *dosa*.   (d) lemon rice and *chikoos*.

(iv) While the train was moving, it suddenly became dark because

(a) the lights went off.   (b) the train was crossing a river.

(c) the Sun went behind a cloud.   (d) the train passed through a tunnel.

(v) At the end of the train journey, Omana's family will go to.

(a) Kozhikode   (b) Kottayam

(c) *Valiyamma's* house   (d) *Ammumma's* village

2. Write 'T' for True and 'F' for False statements.

(i) To cross the river, cars and the train used separate bridges.

(ii) Some tunnels go completely through mountains.

(iii) People in Udipi wear the same types of clothes as in Ahmedabad.

(iv) There was much smoke and noise at the level crossing.

(v) The fields in Goa are brown and dry.

3. Fill in the blanks.

(i) Some people were going ____________ the bars of the level ____________ .

(ii) The sound of the train's movement changed when they crossed a ____________ on a

____________ .

(iii) On the journey from Goa to Kerala the train passes over 2000 ____________ and

through 92 ____________ .

(iv) On reaching Kottayam, Omana would have spent ____________ days on the train.

(v) Omana ____________ on the ____________ berth to ____________ comics.

4. Match the pictures in Column A with their descriptions in Column B by drawing lines.

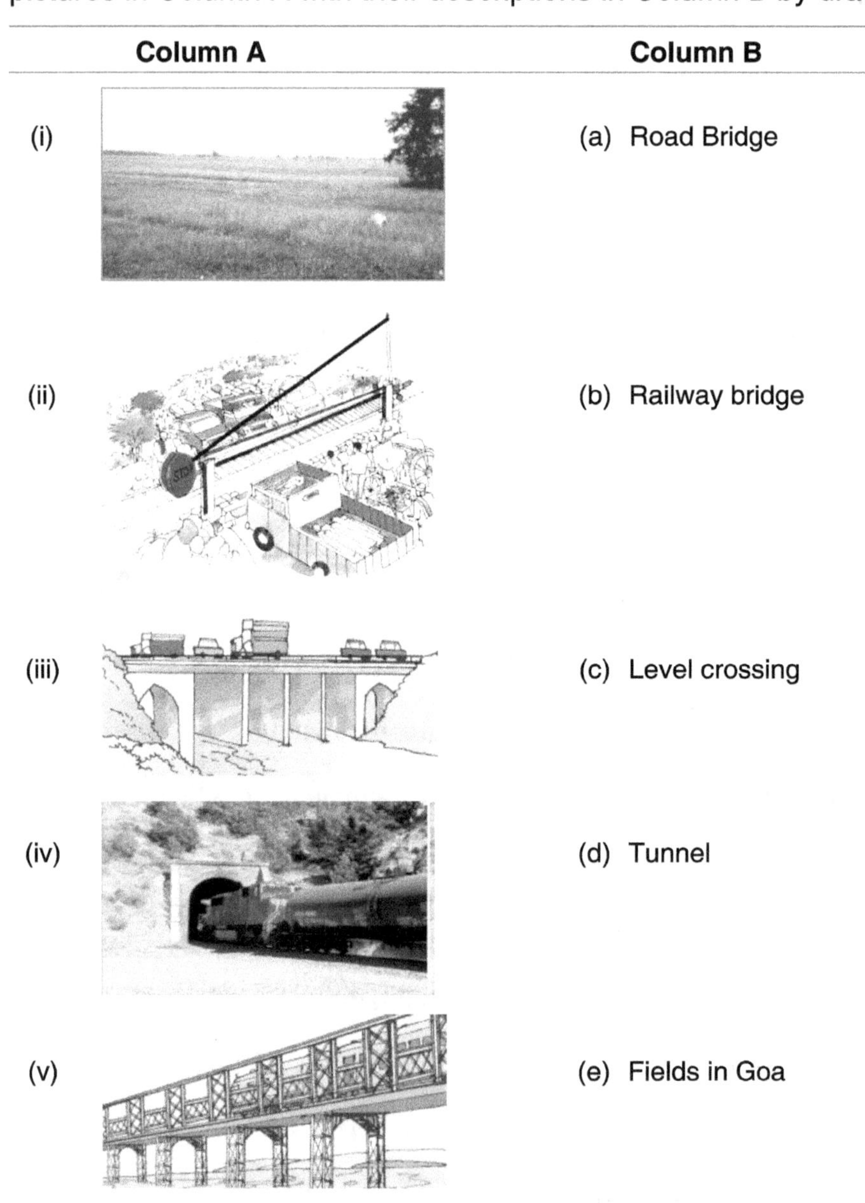

Column A	Column B
(i)	(a) Road Bridge
(ii)	(b) Railway bridge
(iii)	(c) Level crossing
(iv)	(d) Tunnel
(v)	(e) Fields in Goa

5. Match the names of the stations or places in Column A with the time or activity at that place in Column B by drawing arrows.

Column A	Column B
(i) Kottayam	(a) Around 6 o'clock
(ii) Madgaon	(b) Lunch
(iii) Udipi	(c) Late at night
(iv) Kozhikode	(d) Early morning

Very Short Answer Type Question

6. Answer in one word or one sentence.

(i) Why did Omana exchange addresses with Sunil's family?

(ii) At what time did Omana's family start packing up?

(III) Why did the lights come on when the train went through the long tunnel?

(iv) Why did the train wheels make a rattling sound when it was crossing the river?

Short Answer Type Question

7. Answer in 30 – 40 words.

(i) Describe the scenery as it appeared to Omana after the train left Udipi.

(ii) Explain why there was much smoke and noise at the level crossing.

Long Answer Type Question

8. Answer in 80 – 100 words.

Omana has seen people wearing different types of clothes, eat different kinds of food and grow different kinds of crops. Describe these differences.

Think, Find and Write

9. Omana's train passed through the states given in the table below. Complete the table from information given in present and the previous chapter. Some information will have to found out from other places.

S.No.	State	Language spoken	Special food item
(i)	Gujarat		
(ii)	Maharashtra		
(iii)	Tamil Nadu		
(iv)	Andhra Pradesh		
(v)	Punjab		

10. The names of some forms of transport are given below in jumbled form. Write the correct name of the form of transport against each.

(i) ELCCY

(ii) LLOUKBC TRAC

(iii) CETSORO

(iv) OOCCTMYLRE

(v) CRUKT

11. What are the differences between bridges and tunnels? Take examples from your chapter.

Chapter 8

Reaching Grandmother's House

1. Select the best option.

(i) The bus dropped Omana's family at the side of

(a) the road. (b) a river.

(c) a lake. (d) *Ammumma's* village.

(ii) *Ammumma* lived

(a) close to *Valiyamma's* house. (b) at Kottayam.

(c) near a railway station. (d) on an island.

(iii) A railway time table gives information about

(a) the route of the trains.

(b) the arrival and departure time at each station.

(c) the stations along the route.

(d) All of these.

(iv) Omana's family reached *Ammumma's* place on

(a) 16 May (b) 17 May

(c) 18 May (d) None of these

(v) Which of the following methods of transport was not used by Omana for reaching *Ammumma's* place?

(a) Bus (b) Boat

(c) Aeroplane (d) Train

2. Write 'T' for True and 'F' for False statements.

(i) When travelling by the ferry, the tickets were bought after getting on the boat.

(ii) Omana did not eat on reaching *Valiyamma's* house because she was feeling sleepy.

(iii) Omana's family got off the bus in the middle of its journey.

(iv) Omana saw people waving to her from the banks of the river when she was on the boat.

(v) Omana's journey to *Ammumma's* place was boring.

3. Fill in the blanks.

(i) Omana's family reached her *Ammumma's* place in the __________ .

(ii) Omana's __________ bought tickets for them on the bus.

(iii) Standing by the railing of the boat, Omana saw the __________ of the water when the boat moved.

(iv) __________ family also went with Omana's family to *Ammumma's* place.

(v) Omana's legs were stiff at the end of the bus journey because the journey was __________ .

4. Given below are some events mentioned by Omana in her diary. Put them in the correct sequence by numbering them from 1 to 8.

Number in Sequence

(i) The bus had dropped us by the water side.   __________

(ii) It was time for us to get off.   __________

(iii) I had just fallen asleep when *Amma* woke me up again.   __________

(iv) As it went along, the bus got very crowded.   __________

(v) Everyone had to pay the fare before getting on.   __________

(vi) We reached Kottayam in the night.   __________

(vii) There is the ferry, *Amma* said.   __________

(viii) We also had to share our seats.   __________

5. Match the pictures in Column A with their descriptions in Column B by drawing lines.

Column A	**Column B**

(i)

6335 NAGARCOIL EXPRESS				
S.No Station Name	Arrival Time	Departure Time	Distance (Kilometre)	Day
1. GANDHIDHAM	–	05:15	0	1
2. AHMEDABAD	11:30	11:50	301	1
3. VADODARA	14:03	14:10	401	1
4. SURAT	16:15	16:20	530	1
5. VALSAD	17:23	17:25	598	1
6. BHIWANDI ROAD	21:10	21:12	772	1
7. MADGAON	07:35	07:45	1509	2
8. UDUPI	12:06	12:18	1858	2
9. KOZHIKODE	17:45	17:50	2165	2

(a)   Going to *Valiyamma's* house

(ii)

(b)   Train ticket

(iii)

(c)   Railway time table

(iv)

(d)   On the ferry

Very Short Answer Type Question

6. Answer in a few words or one sentence.

(i) Why did Omana's family have to share their seats in the bus?

(ii) Why is ferry used by the people?

(iii) Why was Omana feeling sleepy when they reached *Valiyamma's* house?

(iv) What three forms of transport did Omana use to reach *Ammumma's* place?

(v) How did Omana reach *Valiyamma's* house from Kottayam railway station?

Short Answer Type Question

7. Answer in 30 – 40 words.

(i) What did Omana see on the banks of the river when she stood at the railing?

(ii) What information does the train ticket given in the textbook tell about the passengers?

Long Answer Type Question

8. Answer in 80 – 100 words.

Omana has described her journey to *Ammumma's* place as 'interesting'. Write the points of the journey which Omana found interesting.

Think, Find and Write

9. See the time table of the train given in the textbook, which shows many stations where Omana's train stopped. Omana has not mentioned many of these stations in her diary. Write down those station names along with the day of their departure?

Chapter 9

Changing Families

1. Select the best option.

  (i) Nimmi has now got a

    (a) baby sister   (b) baby brother

    (c) new toy   (d) new mother

  (ii) The number of people in Nimmi's family are now

    (a) four   (b) five

    (c) six   (d) not known

  (iii) __________ father has been promoted.

    (a) Nimmi's   (b) Tsering's

    (c) Nazli's   (d) None of these

  (iv) Tsering's father is going to work in another city because of his

    (a) transfer   (b) promotion

    (c) Both (a) and (b)   (d) Neither (a) nor (b)

  (v) Nazli's __________ is getting married.

    (a) younger brother   (b) father's younger brother

    (c) uncle   (d) elder cousin brother

2. Write 'T' for True and 'F' for False statements.

  (i) Tsering and his mother are going with his father to the new city.

  (ii) Nazli is sad that her cousin brother is getting married and going away.

  (iii) Nimmi's baby sister was born at home.

  (iv) Tsering's mother and sister packed the luggage carefully.

  (v) Nimmi's uncle is blind.

3. Match the persons in Column A with what is happening to them (Activities) in Column B.

Column A	Column B
(i) Nimmi	(a) gets married
(ii) Nazli	(b) becomes a mother again
(iii) Tsering	(c) gets transferred
(iv) Nimmi's mother	(d) is very excited
(v) Nazli's elder cousin brother	(e) will have to attend another school
(vi) Tsering's father	(f) is happy to attend a marriage in the family

4. In Nimmi's family tree shown below, only Nimmi's name is filled in. Fill in the numbered boxes with the names given on the side correctly.

Nimmi's baby sister

Nimmi's mother

Grandmother

Nimmi's uncle

Nimmi's father

Very Short Answer Type Question

5. Answer in one word or one sentence.

(i) Why do many girls drop out of school, as mentioned in the chapter?

(ii) What change occurred in Nimmi's family?

(iii) Why was Tsering's father transferred?

(iv) How has Nazli's family changed?

(v) Susheela, who is going back to school after marriage, belongs to which district?

Short Answer Type Question

6. Answer in 30 – 40 words.

(i) Why do married girls want to go back to finish school? Who helps them in this task?

(ii) How Susheela got the help from the Panchayat?

Long Answer Type Question

7. Answer in 80-100 words.

What were the reasons for changes occurring in Nimmi, Tsering and Nazli's families?

Think, Find and Write

8. Fill in the table on celebration of important days / festivals by ticking the correct boxes (only one box in each row is to be ticked).

Name of Days / Festivals	Normally celebrated at home with the family and friends	Normally celebrated in school with teachers and classmates	May be celebrated at both places
New Year's Day			
Republic Day			
Holi			
Eid			
Independence Day			
Gandhi Jayanti			
Diwali			
Guru Nanak's birthday			
Christmas			

9. Find out and write whether you have a joint family or a nuclear family. Then draw a family tree of your present family.

Hu Tu Tu, Hu Tu Tu

1. Select the best option.

(i) A Kabaddi team has ___________ players.

    (a) five   (b) six

    (c) seven   (d) None of these

(ii) In Kho-Kho, what happens when someone touches you?

    (a) No points are counted   (b) The game ends

    (c) You remain in the game   (d) You get 'out'

(iii) Karnam Malleshwari lives in

    (a) Andhra Pradesh   (b) Mumbai

    (c) Delhi   (d) None of these

(iv) Jwala, Leela and Heera have been

    (a) Kabaddi coaches   (b) Kho-kho coaches

    (c) Kabaddi players   (d) All of these

(v) All games have rules which every ___________ should follow .

    (a) referee   (b) spectator

    (c) player   (d) None of these

2. Write 'T' for True and 'F' for False statements.

(i) Rosy was in Shyamala's team.

(ii) Six players got out when Shyamala touched the line.

(iii) You have to use both your mind and body while playing Kabaddi.

(iv) Karnam Malleshwari started weight lifting from the age of ten.

(v) Jwala and Leela's parents did not allow them to play Kabaddi.

3. Fill in the blanks.

(i) ______________ played Kabaddi during her childhood.

(ii) ______________ father works in the police.

(iii) ______________ managed to touch the centre line.

(iv) ______________ said that her team was not 'out'.

(v) ______________ wishes that children play games, especially Kabaddi.

Very Short Answer Type Questions

4. Answer the questions given below on the picture shown in one word each.

(i) Name the girl whose T-shirt has the number 2.

____

(ii) How many girls are in her opposing team?

____

(iii) What game are they playing?

____

5. Answer in one sentence each.

(i) What made Jwala, Leela and Heera famous?

____

(ii) Name one game besides Kabaddi where it is important to touch a player.

____

(iii) Why was it important for Shyamala to hold her breath until she had touched the centre line?

____

(iv) How much weight can Karnam Malleshwari lift?

(v) Who encouraged Jwala, Leela and Heera to play Kabaddi?

Short Answer Type Question

6. Answer in 30 – 40 words.

(i) What two things did Shyamala do to win the game?

(ii) How did Karnam Malleshwari become famous?

(iii) What two reasons were given by Jwala for people stopping girls from playing Kabaddi?

Long Answer Type Question

7. Answer in 80 – 100 words.

Describe what happened when Leela and Heera decided to watch a movie before an important match.

Think, Find and Write

8. Some games and sports like Kho-Kho and Kabaddi require players to touch other players. Other games do not require or allow a player to touch other players. Name at least three such outdoor games which are played even by children of your age.

9. What is Kabaddi? Write some points by taking help from your NCERT book.

Chapter 11

The Valley of Flowers

1. Select the best option.

   (i) ___________ is prepared from flowers.

     (a) *Itr* ☐   (b) Rose water ☐

     (c) *Kewra* water ☐   (d) All of these ☐

  (ii) Madhubani is

     (a) a place famous for its paintings. ☐   (b) a place famous for preparing perfumes. ☐

     (c) a place famous for its sweets. ☐   (d) None of these. ☐

 (iii) In UP, vegetables for eating are made out of ___________ flowers.

     (a) *sahjan* ☐   (b) *kachnar* ☐

     (c) banana ☐   (d) rose ☐

 (Iv) In the Valley of Flowers, the flowers bloom

     (a) all round the year ☐   (b) only in summer ☐

     (c) for a few weeks in the year ☐   (d) in spring ☐

  (v) Plucking a flower means

     (a) picking it up from the ground ☐   (b) breaking it from a plant ☐

     (c) removing it from a bouquet ☐   (d) All of these ☐

2. Write 'T' for True and 'F' for False statements.

   (i) The Valley of Flowers is in the plains of Uttarakhand state. ☐

  (ii) Flowers grow from fruits also. ☐

 (iii) Flowers are used for making medicines. ☐

 (iv) Colour made from the marigold flower cannot be used to dye cloth. ☐

  (v) Paintings can be made from paste of powdered rice. ☐

3. Fill in the blanks.

(i) We can see flowers growing on _____________ , _____________ , _____________ and

_____________ .

(ii) Some flowers bloom only in the _____________ and close at _____________ .

(iii) In Kerala, people eat vegetables made from _____________ flowers .

(iv) Songs are sung on _____________ during weddings and festivals.

(v) A design of flowers made on clothes is called a _____________ design.

(vi) _____________ district in UP is famous for *Itr*.

Very Short Answer Type Question

4. Answer the questions given below

(i) What is *Itr?*

(ii) Give two uses of rose water.

(iii) Name any three festivals when flowers are used.

Short Answer Type Questions

5. Answer in 30 – 40 words.

(i) What are the uses of flowers in our daily life?

(ii) In what forms can flowers be eaten? Give three examples from states of India where they are eaten.

(iii) How do we prepare 'Granny's recipe' to prevent our skin from cracking during winter?

(iv) What is so special about the colours used in Madhubani paintings?

6. Name the flowers described below (in some cases, there may be more than one).

(i) Changes its direction to always face the sun.

(ii) Having thorns on its tree.

7. Answer the following questions based on the picture given below.

(i) What is the boy doing?

(ii) Why should the boy not do this? Instead, from where should he get what he wants?

8. After the flowers used in garlands, bouquets and vases have dried up, what is best way to put them to further use?

9. Discuss how flowers are important in our life in five points?

Think, Find and Write

10. With the help of your elders, write some points about how we should care the flower plants?

Chapter 12

Changing Times

1. Select the best option.

   (i) What did Chetandas do when his father and mother were making their first house in Sohna village?

       (a) He gave the earth dug by *Baba* to *Amma*.

       (b) He encouraged them.

       (c) He brought tea and snacks for them.

       (d) He looked after his baby sister.

   (ii) Chetandas liked his house the best because

       (a) it was built by his *Baba* and *Amma*.　　(b) it was better than the other houses.

       (c) it was just like their earlier house.　　(d) All of these.

   (iii) When Chetandas was to get married, another room was made using walls of

       (a) iron and cement.　　(b) unbaked bricks.

       (c) baked bricks.　　(d) gunny bags covered with mud.

   (iv) When Raju got married, the family used ___________ for a roof.

       (a) a lintel　　(b) marble chips and cement

       (c) coloured tiles　　(d) None of these

   (v) Where does Suman and her husband stay nowadays?

       (a) Palwal　　(b) Sohna

       (c) Delhi　　(d) Both (b) and (c)

2. Write 'T' for True and 'F' for False statements.

   (i) When Chetandas got married, the entire family used to eat their meals in the kitchen.

   (ii) When Raju got married, the family built an extra room to welcome the new bride.

   (iii) Presently Chetandas writes about the days of his childhood.

(iv) Montu lives in a high-rise building in Delhi.

(v) Chetandas' job in Dera Gazikhan was to teach children.

3. Fill in the blanks.

(i) Termites do not damage wood if branches of _______ are put on it.

(ii) The toilet in the family's first house in Sohna was made out of _______ behind _______.

(iii) At the time of Raju's marriage, they put _______ to take away the waste.

(iv) When Chetandas' family moved from Pakistan to India, they stayed in _______ in a camp.

(v) The floor of the family's first house in Sohna was coated with a mixture of _______ to keep _______ away.

4. Match the pictures shown in Column A with their descriptions in Column B by drawing lines.

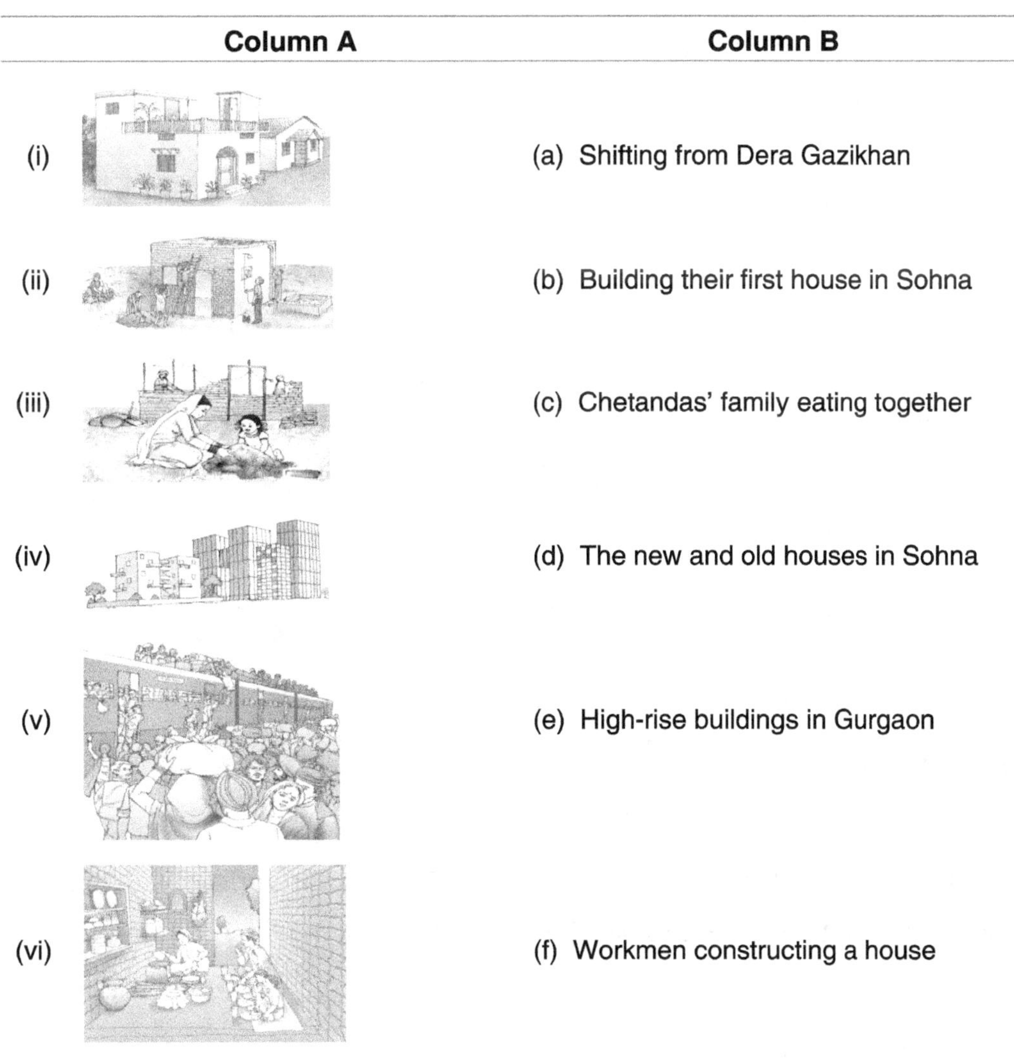

Column A	Column B
(i)	(a) Shifting from Dera Gazikhan
(ii)	(b) Building their first house in Sohna
(iii)	(c) Chetandas' family eating together
(iv)	(d) The new and old houses in Sohna
(v)	(e) High-rise buildings in Gurgaon
(vi)	(f) Workmen constructing a house

Very Short Answer Type Questions

5. Different kinds of skilled persons are required for construction of a house or building. These persons are given in the table below. Find out what work they do and fill up the table.

Name of Person	Work that the person does
Architect	
Plumber	
Electrician	
Mason	
Bricklayer	
Carpenter	
Painter	

6. How did different people in Sohna go for their toilet in the beginning?

Short Answer Type Questions

7. Chetandas made changes in his house whenever there was a change in his family. In the table given below, fill in the columns regarding the changes made and material used.

Change in family condition	Change in house	New material used	Change in kitchen	Change in toilet
Shifting from Dera Gazikhan				
Building house in Sohna village				
When Chetandas got married				
His son Raju got married				
Raju renovated the house				

8. India was divided into India and Pakistan in 1947 when Chetandas was nine years old. He says that now he is 70 years old. Calculate the year in which Chetandas has written this story.

9. Why did the family have to move from their village over sixty years ago?

____

Long Answer Type Question

10. Answer in 30 – 40 words.

   (i) What work did each member of the family do when they built their first house in Sohna?

____

____

   (ii) What changes were done when Raju was to get married.

____

____

   (ii) After coming to India, Chetandas lived in three types of houses. In all these years he saw many changes in his own house. Every time, whenever there was a change in his family, they brought a change in their house. Complete the table and observe the changing times.

The changing time	Material used	Type of kitchen	Type of toilet
A new home when Chetandas came to India from Pakistan.			
When Chetandas got married.			
When Raju got married.			
When Monty moved to Delhi.			

Think, Find and Write

11. There are many differences between houses made in cities and those built in villages. Write some differences.

____

____

____

Chapter 13

A River's Tale

1. Select the best option.

   (i) River water will not become dirty if you

       (a) bathe in it.   (b) drink it.

       (c) empty waste into it.   (d) wash clothes in it.

   (ii) The colour of water will change if we try to dissolve ___________ in it.

       (a) mustard oil   (b) sugar

       (c) salt   (d) cooking soda

   (iii) ___________ are sources of drinking water.

       (a) Mountains and hills   (b) Cities and villages

       (c) Rivers and lakes   (d) Oceans and seas

   (iv) The colour of river water is ___________ when it comes down from the mountains.

       (a) green   (b) reddish-brown

       (c) the colour of mud   (d) blue

   (v) The water in a river ___________ during the rainy season.

       (a) becomes more dirty   (b) increases

       (c) Both (a) and (b)   (d) Neither (a) nor (b)

2. Write 'T' for True and 'F' for False statements.

   (i) We can drink sea water without harming our health.

   (ii) If we see fish swimming in a river, it means that the water is clean.

   (iii) We should not wash our clothes in the river.

   (iv) Water changes colour after it passes a city because some water is removed for use by people living in the city.

   (v) One of the best ways to clean water is by boiling it.

3. Fill in the blanks.

(i) If many dead fishes are found on the banks of a river, it means that the river water is

_______________ .

(ii) If we try to dissolve *haldi* in water, the water changes colour to _____________ .

(iii) Wheat flour _____________ in water.

(iv) If oil leaks from a ship on the river it may _____________ the fish in the river.

(v) Even if the water appears _____________ it may not be alright to drink.

4. Complete these words given in the chapter by filling letters in the blank spaces using the letters A to Z not more than once in each word.

(i) _I_S_L_E   (ii) S_E_B_T   (iii) _US_A_D _I_   (iv) C_O_IN_

(v) _T_N_I_S   (vi) F_C_O_IE_   (vii) B_T_IN_   (viii) _AS_I_G

(ix) FL_W_N_   (x)_R_N_I_G

Very Short Answer Type Questions

5. Match the items in Column A with information about them in Column B by drawing arrows.

Column A	Column B
(i) Sand	(a) dissolves in water
(ii) Boiling water	(b) pollutes the water used
(iii) Milk	(c) has many fish if it is clean
(iv) Washing clothes	(d) does not dissolve in water
(v) River water	(e) makes it drinkable

6. Answer in one word or one sentence.

(i) Give three reasons which will make river water impure and not fit for drinking?

____

(ii) What are two man-made sources of water?

____

(iii) If we drink dirty water, what can happen to us?

____

(iv) From where does a river usually start and where does it usually end?

____

(v) Why does the colour of river water change from place to place?

____

Short Answer Type Question

7. Answer in 30 – 40 words.

    (i) In a river, some parts have many fish while others have much less fish. Why?

    (ii) How does the water in ponds and lakes become impure?

Long Answer Type Question

8. Discuss the activity by which we can understand how water in river, lakes, etc changes when it flows through different cities or villages?

Think, Find and Write

9. Some activities are given below in jumbled form. Write the correct name of the activity against each.

    (i) AINWHGS EOTLESH

    (ii) TTIIMENG EOKMS

    (iii) AAILMN ABGHINT

    (iv) LIO AEKL

    (v) AMN ABGHITN

10. Due to which activities seen in the drawing shown in Q no. 5 does the river water become impure? In each activity, mention what is added or removed to make it pure.

11. Suggest some changes in the drawing shown in Q no. 5 giving reasons, so that the water entering the sea at the end remains fit for drinking.

12. Find out and write about some methods for saving water. In each method, explain how water is saved.

Chapter 14

Basva's Farm

1. Select the best option.

   (i) The onion seeds were sown in the month of

     (a) June.   (b) July.

     (c) August.   (d) December.

  (ii) The *khunti* is used for.

     (a) planting the soil.   (b) digging and loosening the soil.

     (c) taking out the onions.   (d) watering the crop.

 (iii) The onions took ___________ to start sprouting after the seeds were sown.

     (a) 10 days   (b) 6 weeks

     (c) 3 months   (d) 20 days

 (iv) The onions are ready to be removed from the soil when

     (a) the leaves start turning green.   (b) the onion becomes red in colour.

     (c) the leaves dry up.   (d) the onion becomes visible above the soil.

  (v) We have to be careful while using the *illige* because

     (a) it is delicate.   (b) it can make you ill.

     (c) its blade is very sharp.   (d) None of these.

2. Write 'T' for True and 'F' for False statements.

   (i) Basva does not go to school for some days because he has to help *Appa* sprinkle the seeds.

  (ii) Before taking the harvested onions to market, their leaves must be removed.

 (iii) The *kurige* is a tool used to extract ripe onions from the soil.

 (iv) *Appa* takes the harvested onions to the market on a handcart.

  (v) Many weeds in a field will not allow a crop to grow properly.

3. Match the picture of the tool in Column A with its local name in Column B and the work it does in Column C by drawing lines.

	Column A	Column B	Column C
(i)		*Kurige*	(a) Cutting leaves
(ii)	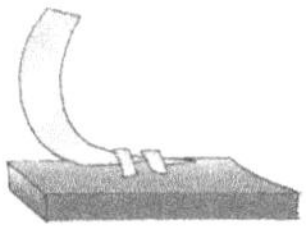	*Khunti*	(b) Making groove in soil for seeds
(iii)	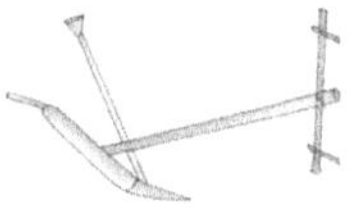	*Illige*	(c) Preparing the soil for sowing seeds

4. Match the pictures in Column A with their descriptions in Column B by drawing lines.

	Column A	Column B
(i)		(a) Digging the soil
(ii)		(b) Planting the seeds
(iii)		(c) Plants are sprouting
(iv)		(d) Removing the weeds
(v)		(e) Harvesting the onion crop
(vi)		(f) Getting the crop ready for the market

5. Fill in the blanks.

    (i) *Appa* planted ______________ in the field.

    (ii) The ____________ is an iron rod used to dig the soil before planting seeds.

    (iii) Basva lives in ____________ village in ____________ state.

    (iv) To have a good crop, it is required to drop ____________ of seeds at ____________ distances.

    (v) ____________ grow alongwith the sprouting onion plants.

Very Short Answer Type Questions

6. Why was Basva's family happy this year?

____

7. Give three uses of *'Khunti'*.

____

8. Why *illige* is used?

____

Short Answer Type Question

9. Answer in 30 – 40 words.

    (i) If the ripe onion crop is not taken out at the right time, what will happen?

____

____

    (ii) Why is it important to remove weeds from the field where the crops are grown?

____

____

    (iii) How will we come to know that onions are ready to be taken out?

____

____

Long Answer Type Question

10. Answer in 80 – 100 words.

Write in the correct order the steps which are required for growing and selling the onion crop, mentioning in each step who are the persons responsible. The last step has been done for you.

Steps	Persons responsible
Take to the big market for selling	*Appa*

Think, Find and Write

11. In India, there are usually two seasons for growing crops, called *rabi* and *kharif*. Find out

   (i) in which months of the year these seasons fall, and

  (ii) which crops in your area are grown in the *rabi* season and the *kharif* season.

Fill up the table below with what you found.

Season	Months in which it falls	Crops grown
Rabi		
Kharif		

12. Basva's father takes the onions to the market in a truck. Find out and write what other means of transport are used by farmers.

13. In this chapter, the steps for growing a vegetable crop are given. Find out from your teacher or elders and write what steps are required for growing (i) a cereal crop like wheat or rice, and (ii) a leguminous crop which gives a *dal.*

Chapter 15

From Market to Home

1. Select the best option.

(i) The vegetable which spoils quickly and has a smooth surface is

(a) potato.

(b) tomato.

(c) onion.

(d) apple.

(ii) The vegetable seller's family has to sort the new vegetables quickly because

(a) the children have to go to school early.

(b) the vegetables should remain fresh.

(c) they have to reach the bazaar early.

(d) All of the above.

(iii) A fruit which spoils quickly and has a rough outside surface is

(a) gourd.

(b) grape.

(c) pineapple.

(d) None of these.

(iv) Water should be sprinkled on the vegetables so that

(a) they do not dry up.

(b) they look good to customers.

(c) they taste better.

(d) All of these.

(v) _____________ is a leafy vegetable.

(a) Brinjal

(b) Carrot

(c) Mango

(d) Spinach

2. Write 'T' for True and 'F' for False statements.

(i) *Chhotu* and Vaishali help *Amma* in sprinkling water on yesterday's unsold vegetables.

(ii) Vaishali's father goes to the *mandi* in a tempo.

(iii) *Babuji* leaves for the bazaar after 9 o'clock in the morning.

(iv) Vaishali gets up early, as she has to reach school on time.

(v) *Babuji* and *Bhaiya* sell all the vegetables that they take to the bazaar.

3. Fill in the blanks.

(i) Vaishali has to reach her school by ____________ .

(ii) The family has their morning tea after taking out the previous day's unsold vegetables from the ____________ .

(iii) Their family looks like a small vegetable market when *Babuji* returns from the ____________ with baskets and sacks full of fresh vegetables.

(iv) If *Babuji* is late in reaching the bazaar, then his ____________ may buy their vegetables from elsewhere.

(v) *Babuji* and *Bhaiya* return from the bazaar at around ____________ .

4. Match the pictures in Column A with their descriptions in Column B by drawing lines.

Column A	Column B
(i)	(a) Sorting yesterday's unsold vegetables
(ii)	(b) Sprinkling water on yesterday's unsold vegetables
(iii)	(c) *Babuji* going to the bazaar
(iv)	(d) *Chhotu* going to school

5. Match the properties/characteristics of vegetables in Column A with their names in Column B by drawing arrows.

Column A	Column B
(i) Fruit which spoils quickly	(a) Ginger
(ii) Vegetable with rough surface	(b) Onion
(iii) Vegetable which spoils quickly	(c) Brinjal
(iv) Vegetable which does not have seeds	(d) Banana
(v) Vegetable with smooth surface	(e) Tomato
(vi) Vegetable which has seeds	(f) Lady finger

Very Short Answer Type Question

6. Answer in one word or one sentence.

(i) What is Vaishali doing at 10 o'clock at night?

(ii) Why does the vegetable seller have to sell the previous day's leftover vegetables first?

(iii) Does *Chhotu* attend school? If so, when does he go?

(iv) Who helps in sorting the vegetables brought from the *mandi* ?

(v) What preparation does the vegetable seller's family make for bringing fresh vegetables from the *mandi* ?

Short Answer Type Question

7. Answer in 30 – 40 words.

(i) Calculate how many hours Vaishali's father remains awake.

(ii) Why do *Babuji* and *Bhaiya* go to the *mandi* early in the morning? Give two reasons.

Long Answer Type Question

8. Answer in 80 – 100 words.

Write the daily activity chart of both Vaishali and *Chhotu* in the table given below, mentioning the time at which each activity takes place, from getting up in the morning to going to sleep at night.

Vaishali's activities		*Chhotu's* activities	
Time	Activity	Time	Activity
3 AM		3 AM	
10 PM		10 PM	

Think, Find and Write

9. Which vegetables can be eaten raw without spoiling our digestion?

____

____

10. Given below are names of some fruits and vegetables. Write their names in your local language.

Fruits		Vegetables	
(a) Apple	_____________	(a) Cauliflower	_____________
(b) Mango	_____________	(b) Onion	_____________
(c) Grapes	_____________	(c) Potato	_____________
(d) Watermelon	_____________	(d) Tomato	_____________
(e) Banana	_____________	(e) Gourd	_____________

Chapter 16

A Busy Month

1. Select the best option.

(i) Birds make nests for

(a) looking after their young.   (b) hatching their eggs.

(c) laying eggs.   (d) All of these

(ii) The Indian robin may build its nest

(a) among stones on the ground.   (b) high up on a tree.

(c) inside a deserted house.   (d) Any of these

(iii) The ____________ lays its eggs inside two leaves it has stitched together.

(a) crow   (b) barbet

(c) *koel*   (d) None of these

(iv) The sunbird makes a nest which

(a) is inside a hole in a tree trunk.   (b) is inside a building.

(c) hangs from a bush.   (d) is made of wire and wood.

(v) ____________ steal bird eggs to eat them.

(a) Cows   (b) Squirrels

(c) Both (a) and (b)   (d) Neither (a) nor (b)

2. Write 'T' for True and 'F' for False statements.

(i) Only the female bird makes the nest.

(ii) The *koel* lays its eggs in another bird's nest.

(iii) Some birds suck nectar from flowers.

(iv) A straight pointed beak in a bird is helpful to tear and eat meat.

(v) Snakes do not use their teeth for chewing their food.

3. Fill in the blanks.

(i) The baby bird in the robin's nest had its beak wide open because it was waiting for _____________ to be given by its mother.

(ii) The _____________ weaver bird make beautifully woven nests.

(iii) The cat's teeth are _____________ so that it can tear and cut meat easily.

(iv) Cows have large and flat teeth on the _____________ of their mouth to _____________ grass.

(v) A curved upper beak in a bird is useful for _____________ seeds.

4. Match the bird in Column A with the description of its nest in Column B by drawing arrows.

Column A		Column B
(i) Indian robin	(a)	Made in a *mehendi* hedge or among thorns of a cactus
(ii) Crow	(b)	Made inside a house
(iii) Dove	(c)	Does not make its own nest
(iv) Pigeon	(d)	Made in a hole in a tree trunk
(v) Barbet	(e)	Made in between stones with grass, covered with soft twigs and roots
(vi) *Koel*	(f)	Made high on a tree with wood and wire

5. Identify the birds shown with their names by drawing lines.

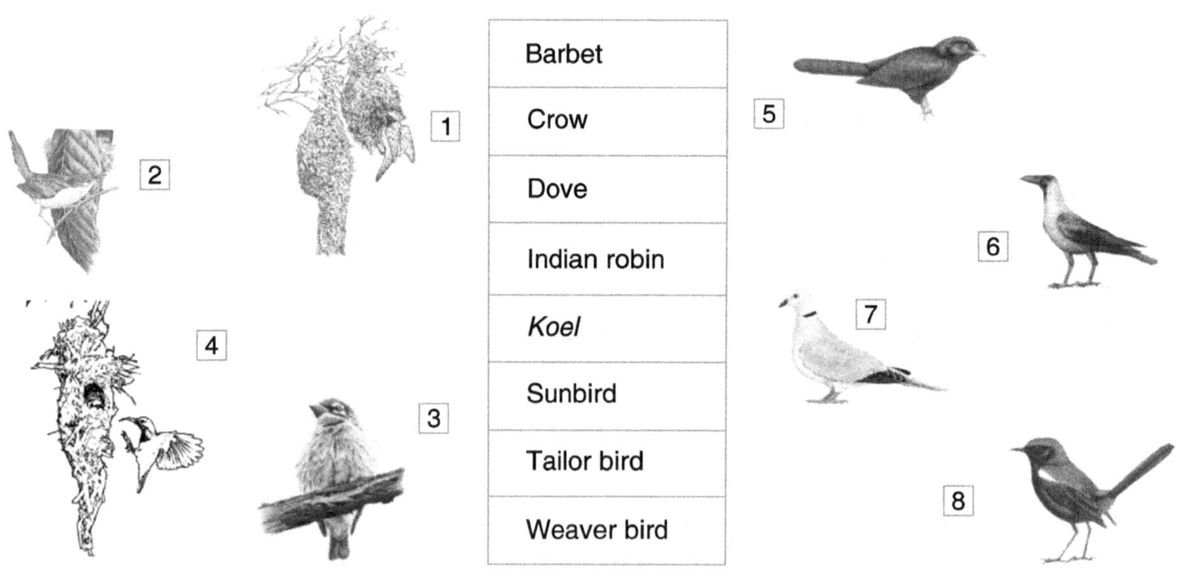

Very Short Answer Type Question

6. Answer in one word or one sentence.

(i) How is Indian robin's nest made?

(ii) Where does the dove make its nest?

(iii) Which creatures are enemies of birds?

(iv) Which bird makes its nest even with spider's cobwebs?

(v) What is odd about squirrel's teeth compared to those of other animals?

Short Answer Type Question

7. Answer in 30 – 40 words.

(i) Why is April a very busy month for birds?

(ii) What is the behaviour of weaver birds when they decide to have a nest for laying eggs?

(iii) How do birds use their nests?

(iv) Fill the following table regarding some animals' teeth – what they are like and what they do.

Name of animal	Description of teeth	What the teeth do
Squirrel		
Cat		
Cow		
Snake		

Long Answer Type Question

8. Answer in 80 – 100 words.

Beaks of the birds vary from one type of bird to another. Write the purposes for which birds use their beaks.

Think, Find and Write

9. Find out and write the names of the birds and animals described below (they are not mentioned in the chapter).

(i) Bird which sleeps during the day but remains awake at night

(ii) National Bird of India

(iii) National Animal of India

(iv) A bird that cannot fly

(v) The bird with the largest egg

10. The names of some birds are given below in jumbled form. Write the correct name of the bird against each.

(i) APSROWR

(ii) AIIDNN BNRIO

(iii) EBBTRA

(iv) ATLIRO DBRI

(v) BNUDRIS

11. Birds do not have teeth, then how do they chew the food that they eat?

Nandita in Mumbai

1. Select the best option.

    (i) We know that Nandita's *Mama's* house had electricity because

        (a) it had a lighted bulb.

        (b) it had a fan which was running.

        (c) his son was watching a TV programme.

        (d) None of the above

    (ii) When Nandita travels by bus to the hospital she knows

        (a) where to get down from the bus.   (b) how much to pay for the ticket.

        (c) how to stand in line.   (d) All of these

    (iii) When Nandita looked down from the window in Babloo's house she could not find out

        (a) her *Mama's* house.   (b) the street in which her *Mama* lived.

        (c) any house.   (d) None of these

    (iv) Nandita's *Mama* had received the notice for leaving their houses _________ in the last ten years .

        (a) twice   (b) three times

        (c) many times   (d) never

    (v) Nandita's *Mami's* work is _________ in seven houses.

        (a) washing utensils   (b) cleaning the house

        (c) Both (a) and (b)   (d) Neither (a) nor (b)

2. Write 'T' for True and 'F' for False statements.

    (i) Nandita travelled every day to see her mother in hospital by the local train.

    (ii) *Mama's* family in Mumbai had seven persons.

(iii) Nandita came to Mumbai for her mother's treatment in a hospital.

(iv) Nandita's house in the village has separate rooms for living, bathing and cooking.

(v) In the village, they always fill water from the river, which is far away.

3. Match the pictures in Column A with their descriptions in Column B by drawing lines.

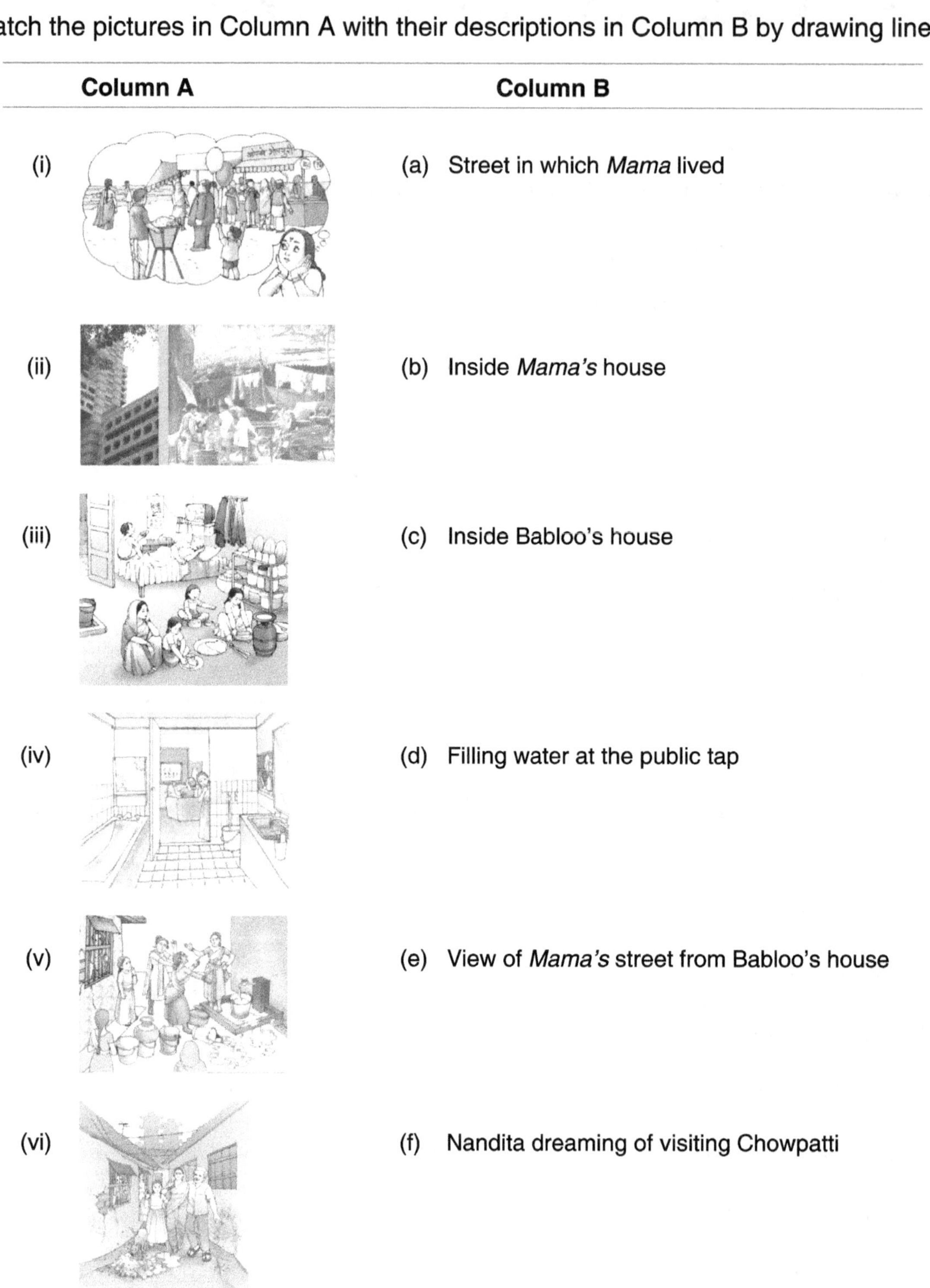

	Column A		Column B
(i)		(a)	Street in which *Mama* lived
(ii)		(b)	Inside *Mama's* house
(iii)		(c)	Inside Babloo's house
(iv)		(d)	Filling water at the public tap
(v)		(e)	View of *Mama's* street from Babloo's house
(vi)		(f)	Nandita dreaming of visiting Chowpatti

4. Fill in the blanks.

(i) The toilet in ____________ is very dirty because everyone in the street uses it and sometimes there is no water.

(ii) ____________ took a long time to clean Babloo's house because it was a big house with many rooms.

(iii) The children near where Nandita stays say that big film stars also came to ____________ .

(iv) ____________ was worried because people asked them to move out from their houses as a big hotel was to be built there.

(v) Nandita became worried and wondered how would she be able to visit her mother every day ____________ .

Very Short Answer Type Question

5. Answer in one word or one sentence.

(i) Why did Nandita close the tap in Babloo's house?

(ii) Why did Nandita catch hold of her mother's hand when they reached Mumbai station?

(iii) Why is Nandita's family not able to fill water for the day if they are just a little late?

(iv) What work does Nandita's *Mami* do?

(v) What facilities are there in the lift, which takes people up and down in the building in which Babloo lives?

Short Answer Type Question

6. Answer in 30 – 40 words.

(i) Why does Nandita's *Mama* have to move out from his house?

(ii) What difficulties will Nandita's *Mama* and *Mami* face if they have to live in another corner of the city?

(iii) What things was Nandita afraid to do when she first came to Mumbai?

Long Answer Type Question

7. Answer in 80 – 100 words.

Describe briefly Nandita's experience of filling water at the public tap in Mumbai. How is this different from getting water for daily needs in the village?

Think, Find and Write

8. What kind of house do you live in? Put a (✓) mark against the right answer.

(a) Nandita's village house   (b) *Mama's* one room house

(c) Big house where *Mami* worked   (d) Babloo's house

(e) Some other type

9. Why is the building in which Babloo lives called a high-rise building?

10. What are the differences between the house of Babloo and the house of Nandita's *Mama*? What are the probable reasons for this?

11. Nandita's *Mama* was living in an area called a 'slum'. What is a slum? Explain briefly.

Chapter 18

Too Much Water, Too Little Water

1. Select the best option.

  (i) The visitor to Suguna's house from the city refused to drink __________ offered to him.

    (a) the glass of water   (b) the cold drink

    (c) the glass of juice   (d) None of these

  (ii) There was a big water park

    (a) near Bazaar Gaon   (b) near Suguna's house

    (c) near Rohan's house   (d) None of these

  (iii) The water park had many

    (a) tall water slides.   (b) water hoses.

    (c) water fountains.   (d) All of these

  (iv) The children in the water park were playing with

    (a) a water hose.   (b) water rides.

    (c) a water slide.   (d) All of these

  (v) The first step taken for solving the water problem in Holgundi was

    (a) making a small dam on the slope.

    (b) planting trees all round it.

    (c) repairing the cracks in the tank.

    (d) cleaning the tank.

2. Write 'T' for True and 'F' for False statements.

   (i) The water available in Nallamada these days is not fit for drinking.

  (ii) The water park had no water to play in but the nearby village had sufficient water.

 (iii) Raziya was worried when she read the newspaper.

 (iv) Raziya planned to clean the water at her home by filtering it.

  (v) We should not take any food when we have diarrhoea.

3. Match the pictures in Column A with their descriptions (Related Activities) in Column B by drawing lines.

Column A	Column B
(i)	(a) Deepak and his mother leaving the lift
(ii)	(b) Rohan's family entering the water park
(iii)	(c) Suguna's father showing water to the visitor
(iv)	(d) Selva bringing a cold drink for the visitor
(v)	(e) Razia Madam talking to Pushpa

4. Match the names of the places in Column A with what happened there in Column B by drawing arrows.

Column A	Column B
(i) Cuffe Parade	(a) The visitor refused the cold drink
(ii) Holgundi	(b) Children play in the water park
(iii) Suguna's village	(c) Deepak's mother took home boiled water for her family
(iv) Bazaar Gaon	(d) Bhima Sangh solved the water problem

5. Fill in the blanks.

   (i) If we drink _________ water we may fall sick of diarrhoea, vomiting etc.

   (ii) The ORS must be sipped _________ by the diarrhoea patients.

   (iii) The ORS prepared by you should not taste more salty than your _________.

   (iv) When we have diarrhoea and vomiting we lose a lot of _________ from our body.

   (v) The village near to the water park had _________ .

   (vi) While preparing ORS, a pinch of salt is to be mixed in boiled and cooled water along with _________ .

   (vii) When the gutter water got mixed with the drinking water pipes, many people became sick with _________ .

   (viii) Suguna's father offered the visitor a cold drink because they were not getting _________ .

Very Short Answer Type Question

6. Answer in one sentence.

   (i) Why was Deepak happy?

   (ii) What was the reason for the villagers making a noise outside the water park?

   (iii) Why did Holgundi not have water shortage earlier?

   (iv) If diarrhoea does not stop after taking medicines and the specially prepared water, what should we do?

   (v) What problems were found by the *Bhima Sangh* in the tank on the hill in Holgundi?

Short Answer Type Question

7. Answer in 30 – 40 words.

   (i) Why did Suguna's father tell the visitor not to drink water in their house?

   (ii) Why was the village Panchayat in Holgundi worried?

   (iii) Two pictures of the water park are given below. What are the differences being shown in the pictures?

Picture 1

Picture 2

Long Answer Type Question

8. Answer in 80 – 100 words.

   (i) Make a list of all the good things that happened after the tank on the hill in Holgundi was repaired and rain started falling.

   (ii) What should be done if a member of our family has diarrhoea and vomiting?

Think, Find and Write

9. How much water do you use in a day and for what purpose? Make a small list?

10. In some seasons of the year you are not allowed to play in a water park. Which are these seasons and why are you not allowed?

11. What are the different ways (besides boiling) by which water is cleaned? Find out and write these ways as given in your chapter.

Chapter 19

Abdul in the Garden

1. Select the best option.

   (i) What vegetables did *Abbu* have to send home?

     (a) Carrot   (b) Radish

     (c) Banyan   (d) Pea

  (ii) Seeds require __________ to germinate and produce roots and a stem.

     (a) air   (b) sunlight

     (c) water   (d) All of these

 (iii) Which of the following vegetables that we eat are actually roots of the plant?

     (a) potato   (b) tomato

     (c) pea   (d) None of these

  (iv) Which of the following things do not grow?

     (a) Leaves   (b) Mosquitoes

     (c) The moon   (d) All of these

   (v) In the Australian desert when there was no water, the local people got water from the __________ of the Desert Oak Tree.

     (a) trunk   (b) roots

     (c) branches   (d) leaves

2. Write 'T' for True and 'F' for False statements.

   (i) Desert Oak tree is found in Indian deserts.

  (ii) Cabbage is a root.

 (iii) Radish and carrot are roots that we eat.

  (iv) Roots help a tree to grow.

   (v) The pea plant has a delicate stem.

3. Fill in the blanks.

(i) ______________ was helping ______________ in the garden.

(ii) The hanging branches of the Banyan tree provide ______________ to the tree.

(iii) Abdul could not pull out the grass plant easily because ______________ and much more spread out than the part of the plant above the ground.

(iv) Despite the strong wind the *neem* tree ______________ on the ground.

(v) The roots of trees go deep into the ground till ______________ .

4. Match the pictures in Column A with their descriptions in Column B by drawing lines.

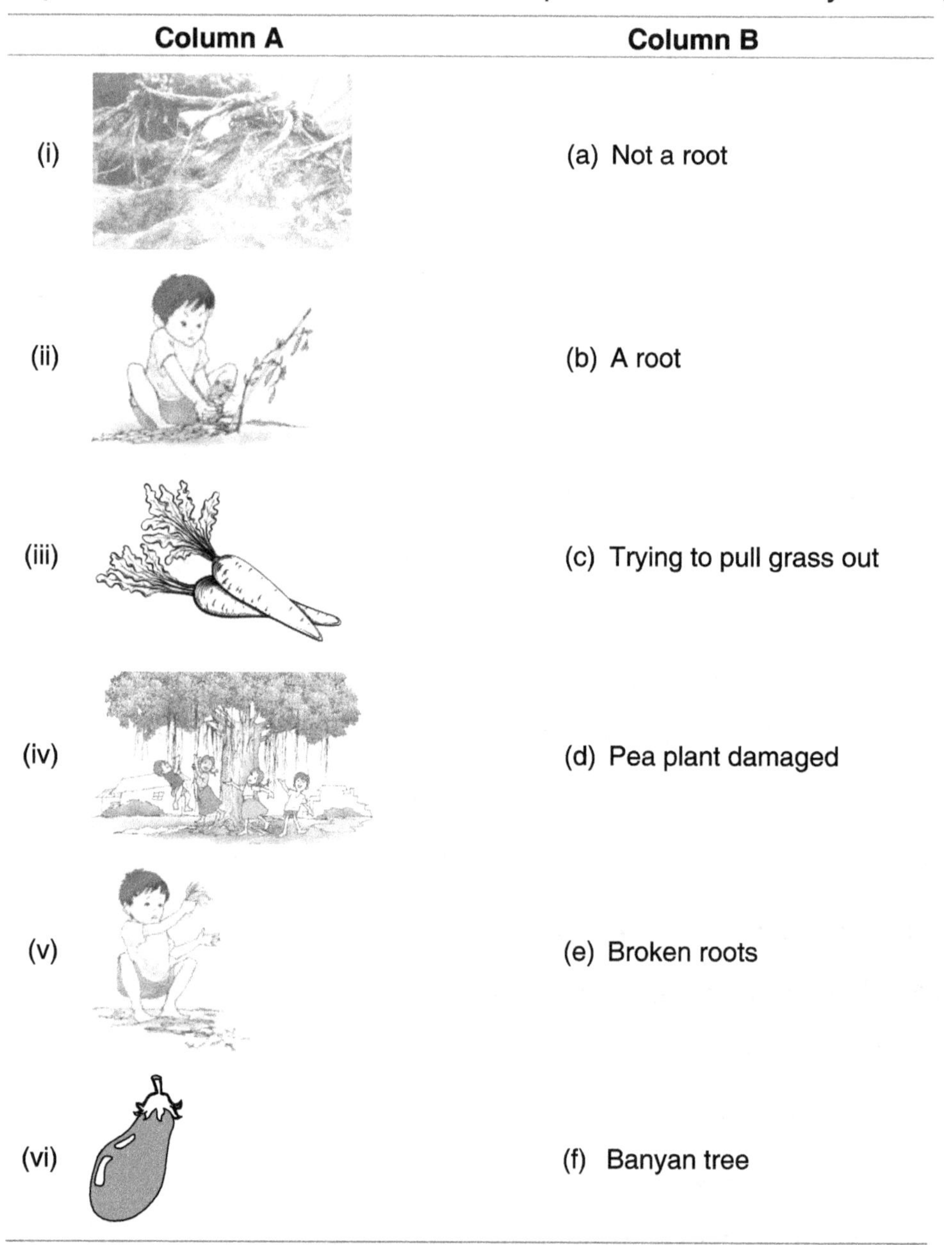

Column A	Column B
(i)	(a) Not a root
(ii)	(b) A root
(iii)	(c) Trying to pull grass out
(iv)	(d) Pea plant damaged
(v)	(e) Broken roots
(vi)	(f) Banyan tree

5. Fill in the blanks by selecting the correct word from those given in brackets.

    (i) The ___________ (potato / carrot) can also be eaten raw.

    (ii) A vegetable with ___________ (rough / smooth) surface is a root.

    (iii) The ___________ (neem / banyan) tree has hanging roots.

    (iv) The ___________ (cotton / desert oak) tree has very long roots.

Very Short Answer Type Questions

6. Answer in one word or one sentence.

    (i) Why was it difficult for Abdul to pull out a small grass plant?

    (ii) Does banyan tree also has roots? If yes, then where?

    (iii) Abdul wondered whether radish was a root. Can you tell why he thought this way?

    (iv) What is the purpose of the hanging branches of a banyan tree?

7. Some words used in the chapter are given below in jumbled form. Write the correct word against each.

    (i) SABELTEGEV

    (ii) EEDRST AKO

    (iii) AGGHNIN OORST

    (iv) DIRHSA

    (v) OOTTNC OOLW

Short Answer Type Question

8. Answer in 30 – 40 words.

  (i) How does a desert oak tree gets water for its roots?

  (ii) Do all plants need water? If so, then what will happen if nobody gives water to these plants?

  (iii) On putting water in the soil where plants are growing, their drooping leaves become fresh again. How?

Long Answer Type Question

9. There is a law against cutting trees. Explain this with an example from your NCERT textbook.

Think, Find and Write

10. The shape of the moon looks different every day. Why does this happen? Take help from your NCERT Book.

11. What happens to very old trees when they die? Do they fall down or do they dry up?

12. You must have seen plants growing from a crack in a wall. How deep must their roots be growing? How do you think its roots get water?

13. What are the differences between living things (like trees and animals) and non-living things (like cars)? Find out and write at least four such differences.

Chapter 20

Eating Together

1. Select the best option.

(i) Aarti enjoyed most __________ at her uncle's wedding.

    (a) having fun   (b) doing everything together

    (c) the wedding feasts   (d) All of these

(ii) While celebrating *Bihu*, everybody danced around the *Bhela Ghar* till

    (a) it was burning.   (b) they were tired.

    (c) the next morning.   (d) night fell.

(iii) *Master Moshai* wanted all the children to __________ before starting to eat.

    (a) sit down in a circle   (b) say their prayers

    (c) wash their hands properly   (d) All of these

(iv) Before eating the midday meal the children

    (a) sat down in a circle.   (b) sang a song together.

    (c) washed their hands properly.   (d) All of these.

(v) The children wish that in the midday meal sometimes they get

    (a) something sweet.   (b) something cold.

    (c) something to drink.   (d) Any of these.

2. Write 'T' for True and 'F' for False statements.

(i) *Bihu* is celebrated after the wheat crop in Assam has been harvested.

(ii) The *Bhela Ghar* is made of grass and bamboo.

(iii) The midday meal was taken in the school at 12 noon.

(iv) Yesterday the school children had *bhat-shukto* for the midday meal.

(v) Outside *Didi Moni's* room, a list of food items has been displayed.

3. Fill in the blanks.

   (i) Aarti put *mehendi* on her palms at _____________ .

  (ii) The midday meal is _____________ right.

 (iii) After _____________ we all stood in queue to take our food.

 (iv) In the midday meal, children should get _____________ food.

  (v) Those children who go to school without eating properly, cannot _____________ .

4. Fill in the blanks with names relating to celebration of the *Bihu* festival.

   (i) The _____________ dish is made from sweet potatoes.

  (ii) _____________ is the first day of the festival, when the whole village eats together.

 (iii) The _____________ is used for cooking *cheva* rice.

 (iv) The women celebrate by dressing in _____________ and _____________ .

5. Match the pictures in Column A with their descriptions in Column B by drawing lines.

Column A	Column B
(i) 	(a) Children practising dancing for *Bihu*
(ii)	(b) *Mezi* on fire
(iii)	(c) School children planning the class party
(iv)	(d) People celebrating *Bihu* festival

Very Short Answer Type Question

6. Answer in one word or one sentence.

(i) What was David's idea about eating and having fun together?

(ii) In which state was *Bihu* being celebrated?

(iii) What is the meaning of *Uruka*?

(iv) Why were the children not able to pay attention to the lesson in the class?

(v) Why did the children want to have a class party?

(vi) What is *tao*?

Short Answer Type Question

7. Answer in 30 – 40 words.

(i) What did Rehana say about parties in her colony?

(ii) When and why did Reena want to have the class party?

(iii) How is *cheva* rice prepared?

Long Answer Type Question

8. Answer in 80 – 100 words.

   (i) Describe what happened at the children's party in the school.

   (ii) Describe the contributions the people make for preparation of the feast celebrating the *Bihu* festival.

Think, Find and Write

9. In which month do the Assamese people normally celebrate the *Bihu* festival? Why is it celebrated?

Chapter 21

Food and Fun

1. Select the best option.

(i) ___________ studied in boarding school.

    (a) Manpreet and Gurnoor   (b) Manjit and Gurnoor

    (c) Swastik and Divya   (d) None of these

(ii) The vegetables being cooked in the Gurudwara were

    (a) potatoes.   (b) cauliflowers.

    (c) Both (a) and (b).   (d) Neither (a) nor (b).

(iii) Where is food cooked at Gurudwara?

    (a) Store   (b) Tandoor

    (c) Angeethi   (d) Microwave

(iv) *Ghee* is applied to the *chapaties*

    (a) when they are rolled.   (b) when they put on the *tava.*

    (c) when the flour is made ready.   (d) when they are taken off the *tava.*

(v) Whose father was Manjit?

    (a) Gurnoor   (b) Divya

    (c) Swastik   (d) All of these

2. Write 'T' for True and 'F' for False statements.

(i) Divya and Swastik came from their home the previous day.

(ii) Divya did not miss her parents when she was in the hostel.

(iii) To make the *kadhah prasad*, flour is fried in the *kadhai.*

(iv) Divya helped in preparing *chapaties* at the Gurudwara.

(v) The *kadhah prasad* was distributed after *ardaas.*

3. Fill in the blanks.

   (i) Manpreet's parents were at ___________ when Divya and Swastik visited them.

   (ii) A lot of ___________ was going on in the Gurudwara when the children reached there.

   (iii) When the children entered the Gurudwara kitchen they saw ___________ boiling.

   (iv) All the people in the Gurudwara sat on *durries* to have ___________.

   (v) The people who served the food in the Gurudwara ate ___________.

   (vi) *Chapaties* are made from ___________.

   (vii) The *kadhah prasad* is a kind of ___________.

4. Match the pictures in Column A with their descriptions (Activities) in Column B by drawing lines.

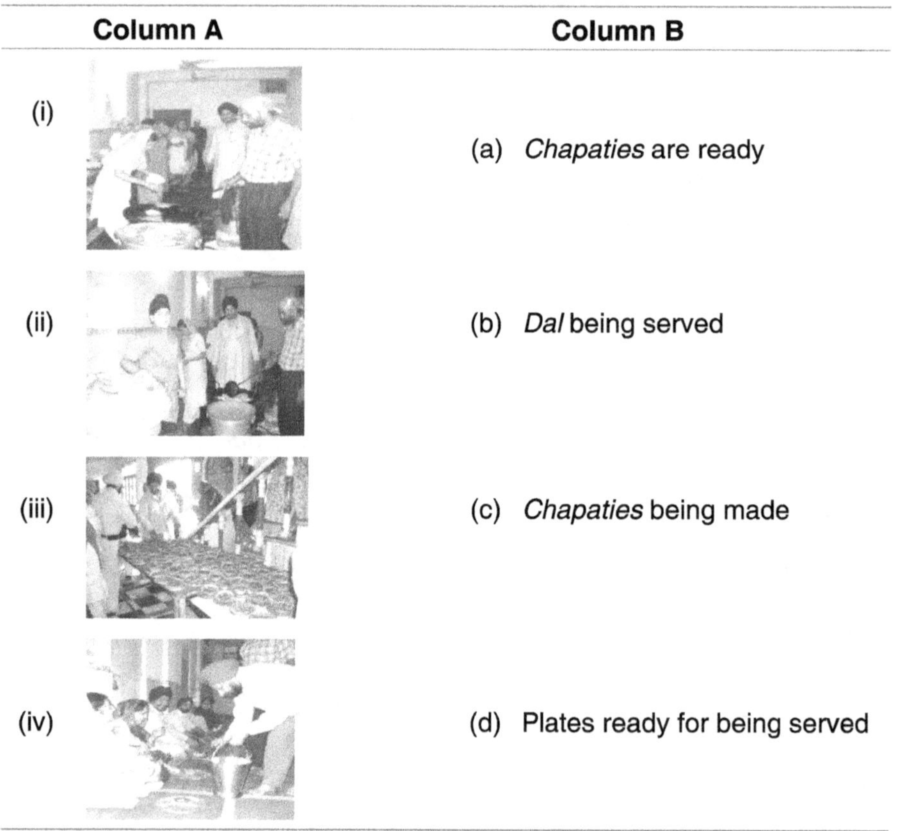

Column A	Column B
(i)	(a) *Chapaties* are ready
(ii)	(b) *Dal* being served
(iii)	(c) *Chapaties* being made
(iv)	(d) Plates ready for being served

Very Short Answer Type Question

5. Answer in one word or one sentence.

   (i) What was Gurnoor's mother doing when the children met her?

____

(ii) What happens when someone in Swastik's hostel gets home-made food?

(iii) Why does Divya say, 'hostel life is fun'?

(iv) Had Swastik ever cooked food before he visited the Gurudwara?

(v) What is *kadhah prasad?*

Short Answer Type Question

6. Answer in 30 – 40 words.

(i) Name the food items prepared in the Gurudwara.

(ii) Who arranges all the material to cook so much food in the Gurudwara?

(iii) After washing hands, what was Divya doing?

Long Answer Type Question

9. Answer in 80 – 100 words.

Describe what was happening in the kitchen of the Gurudwara when the children reached there.

Think, Find and Write

10. Find out and write whether such a tradition of cooking and serving food is followed in temples, churches or mosques, similar to Gurudwaras? What are the occasions when this is done?

Chapter 22

The World in my Home

1. Select the best option.

  (i) Marietta likes to watch __________ while Susan's favourite programme is about __________ .

    (a) cartoons, songs   (b) cartoons, a serial

    (c) songs, cartoons   (d) a film, songs

 (ii) Pratibha feels that the rules should not be __________ for boys and girls.

    (a) the same   (b) similar

    (c) strict   (d) different

(iii) What did the children at the beach learn from Pilloo Aunty's action?

    (a) Excuse the *kulfi*-seller for his mistake.

    (b) You should pay for all the *kulfis* you have eaten.

    (c) You should be honest and fair.

    (d) None of the above.

 (iv) Dhondu thought that his elder uncle's behaviour was

    (a) due to his old age   (b) hindering his progress

    (c) correct   (d) helping him

  (v) Ritu refused to visit Meena's home because

    (a) she do not want chocolates   (b) she was tired

    (c) she scared of her uncle   (d) None of these

2. Write 'T' for True and 'F' for False statements.

  (i) Everyone in Marietta's family had to watch the TV serial that her aunty enjoyed.

 (ii) Pratibha knows that even if her brothers are late reaching home, nobody will scold them.

(iii) Pilloo Aunty paid for all the *kulfis* that they ate.

(iv) Akshay's grandmother did not want him to eat or drink anything at Anil's house. ☐

(v) Her uncle told Meena to bring Ritu home so that he can play with them. ☐

3. Match the pictures in Column A with their descriptions (Related Person) in Column B by drawing lines.

	Column A		Column B
(i)	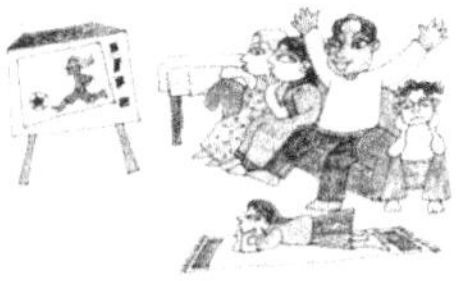	(a)	Anil and Akshay
(ii)	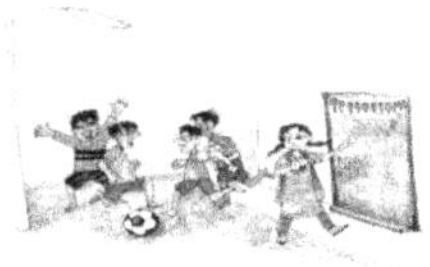	(b)	Ritu and Meena
(iii)	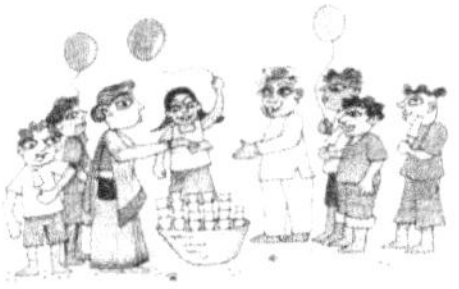	(c)	Dhondu with his uncle
(iv)	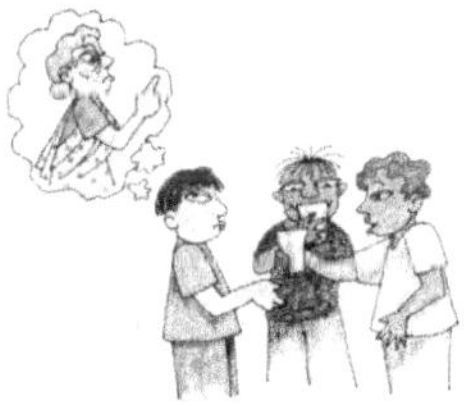	(d)	Pratibha, Sandeep and Sanjay
(v)	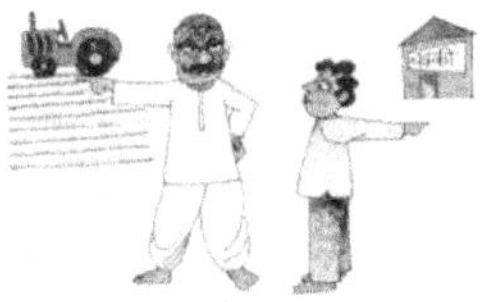	(e)	Meena's uncle
(vi)	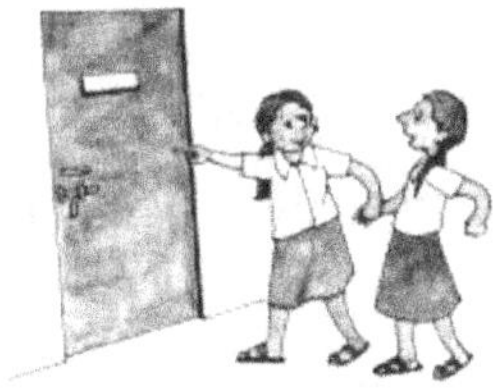	(f)	Marietta's family
(vii)	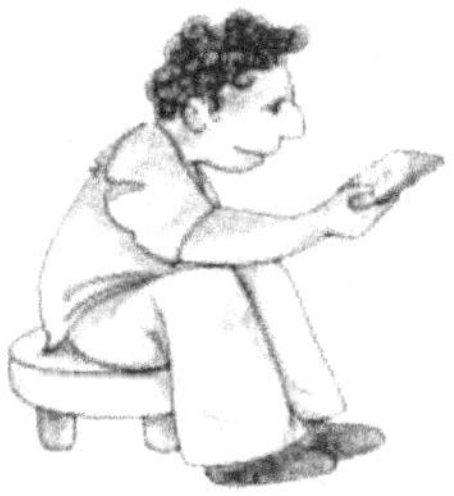	(g)	At the beach

4. Fill in the blanks.

   (i) Marietta's mummy and aunty are good friends but their favourite ___________ are different.

   (ii) At 7 PM, Pratibha finished ___________ and went back home.

   (iii) The *kulfi*-seller asked Pilloo Aunty to pay for ___________ .

   (iv) Dhondu has always worked in the fields, but now he wants to buy a *chakki* machine to ___________ .

   (v) Meena and Ritu were going home after playing ___________ .

Very Short Answer Type Question

5. Answer in one word or one sentence.

   (i) Why was Pratibha hurrying home?

   (ii) Why did the children at the beach think that they had saved some money?

   (iii) Why did Akshay not want to drink water at Anil's house?

   (iv) Why could Dhondu not do what he wanted to do?

Short Answer Type Question

6. Answer in 30 – 40 words.

   (i) What TV programmes did the different people in Marietta's family want to watch?

   (ii) What did Phali, Nazu and their friends do at the beach?

   (iii) Why did Dhondu want to buy a *chakki* machine? Give two reasons.

Long Answer Type Question

7. Answer in 80 – 100 words.

What happened when Anil invited all his friends and Akshay too?

Think, Find and Write

8. What similar problems do you find after reading the different stories in this chapter?

9. Have you ever been stopped by your parents from playing with some kinds of children? What kind of children were they? What reason did your parents give for stopping you? Do you think it was right?

10. In Akshay and Anil's story, at the end it is not written whether Akshay drank the glass of water offered by Anil. If you were Anil, what would you have thought about Akshay if he had refused your offer of water?

Chapter 23

Pochampalli

1. Select the best option.

(i) ____________ before actually weaving the cloth.

    (a) Many different things have to be done

    (b) The looms have to be cleaned

    (c) The threads have to be straightened

    (d) The cotton and silk have to be separated

(ii) ____________ works to dye the thread with bright colours.

    (a) Mother   (b) Father

    (c) Everybody   (d) Prasad

(iii) Silk is becoming ____________ day by day.

    (a) harder to find   (b) more difficult to weave

    (c) more expensive   (d) All of these.

(iv) Big shopkeepers sell the sarees at ____________ prices.

    (a) reasonable   (b) very high

    (c) very low   (d) None of these.

(v) Many craftsmen are leaving their villages to work as ____________ in big cities.

    (a) clerks   (b) weavers

    (c) craftsmen   (d) labourers

2. Write 'T' for True and 'F' for False statements.

(i) Mukhtapur village is in the Pochampalli district of Karnataka.

(ii) Prasad learnt the skill of weaving from his school teacher.

(iii) Silk cloth is woven in looms.

(iv) Silk cloth and silk sarees are woven from silk thread.

(v) Weavers do not get a good price for their hard labour.

3. Match the pictures in Column A with the steps in making Pochampalli sarees described in Column B by drawing lines.

Column A	Column B
(i)	(a) Father brings bundles of thread from Pochampalli city
(ii)	(b) Threads are dyed and rolled into bundles
(iii)	(c) Bundles are put onto looms
(iv)	(d) Cloth is woven
(v)	(e) Finished sarees

4. Fill in the blanks using the correct options from those given in brackets.

(i) The newly bought threads are first put in ___________ (boiling/cold) water to remove dirt and stains.

(ii) The threads are rolled into bundles after ___________ (wetting/drying) them.

(iii) The cloth is woven after the bundles of ___________ (needle/thread) are put onto looms.

(iv) Great skill is needed to weave special ___________. (sheets/sarees)

(v) ___________ (Silk/Cotton) thread is used to weave sheets.

(vi) Pochampalli sarees have ___________ (bright/dull) colours.

(vii) Size and number of ___________ (threads/needles) change according to the design.

Very Short Answer Type Questions

5. Answer in one word or one sentence.

(i) How did Pochampalli cloth get its name?

____

(ii) Why does the loom need many needles?

____

(iii) Why is Vani's home always filled with brightly coloured threads?

____

(iv) From where did Vani's parents learn to make such beautiful sarees?

____

6. Complete these words or phrases given in the chapter by filling letters in the blank spaces using the letters A to Z not more than once in each word.

(i) _H_E_D   (ii) T_A_IT_ON_L

(iii) _E_VI_G   (iv) BU_D_E_

(v) _H_PK_E_E_S   (vi) P_E_I_US

(vii) _O_LI_G _A_ER   (viii) _U_L_ _HA_LS

(ix) _O_H__PA_L_   (x) M_K_TA_U_

Short Answer Type Question

7. Answer in 30 – 40 words.

   (i) Why are many weavers giving up this craft which has been done by their family members for generations?

Long Answer Type Question

8. Answer in 80 – 100 words.

   (i) Briefly describe how a Pochampalli saree is made from buying the threads to finishing the saree.

   (ii) Explain why this family craft of making sarees is in danger of being lost forever.

Think, Find and Write

9. Names of some traditional Indian crafts are given below in jumbled form. Write their correct name against each.

   (i) EYRTOTP

   (ii) AKSBRROSW

   (iii) YTO AGIKMN

   (iv) AECTPR AEGINVW

   (v) DOWO ACGINVR

10. How are traditional arts and crafts continued for many years?

11. In the practice of many traditional crafts, the entire family participates. Why do you think this is necessary?

Chapter 24

Home and Abroad

1. Select the best option.

(i) *Chittappan* had got a job in ___________ five years ago.

(a) Kerala ☐ (b) Chennai ☐

(c) Abu Dhabi ☐ (d) Dubai ☐

(ii) In Abu Dhabi there is a lot of ___________ under the sandy soil.

(a) oil ☐ (b) water ☐

(c) coal ☐ (d) All of these ☐

(iii) Mountains made only of sand are called

(a) sand hills. ☐ (b) desert hills. ☐

(c) sand dunes. ☐ (d) desert dunes. ☐

(iv) The only kind of trees Sashi saw in Abu Dhabi were ___________ trees.

(a) coconut ☐ (b) date palm ☐

(c) jackfruit ☐ (d) betel nut ☐

(v) The money used in Abu Dhabi is called

(a) Dollar. ☐ (b) Pound. ☐

(c) Rupee. ☐ (d) Dirham. ☐

2. Write 'T' for True and 'F' for False statements.

(i) Shanta was tired after the long flight from Abu Dhabi. ☐

(ii) Shanta said that Abu Dhabi is far from India. ☐

(iii) It rains often in Abu Dhabi. ☐

(iv) Buildings in Abu Dhabi are air conditioned. ☐

(v) People in Abu Dhabi usually wear woollen clothes. ☐

3. Fill in the blanks.

(i) Maalu and her father went to the airport to receive __________ .

(ii) *Kunjamma* was the wife of __________ .

(iii) Maalu's cousins were named __________ and __________ .

(iv) The places Maalu found on the globe were, __________, __________, __________ and __________ .

(v) Water is very __________ in desert areas.

4. Match the name of the country in Column A with the picture of its currency in Column B by drawing arrows.

Column A		Column B
(i) USA	(a)	Picture 1
(ii) India	(b)	Picture 2
(iii) Oman	(c)	Picture 3
(iv) People's Republic of China	(d)	Picture 4
(v) England	(e)	Picture 5

Very Short Answer Type Question

5. Answer in one word or one sentence.

   (i) Why was there a lot of activity at Maalu's house today?

   (ii) Why were Shanta and Sashi surprised?

   (iii) What did *Chittappan* give Maalu?

   (iv) Why did *Chittappan* say that in Abu Dhabi they could not open the house windows?

   (v) What did Maalu decide to do for her class?

Short Answer Type Question

6. Answer in 30 – 40 words.

   (i) Describe what interesting things Shanta saw from the plane during the flight.

   (ii) Describe the gifts *Kunjamma* gave everyone.

   (iii) How do people living in Abu Dhabi protect themselves from the heat?

   (iv) *Chittappan* said that 'In fact, petrol is cheaper than water.' Why did he say so?

Long Answer Type Question

7. Answer in 80 – 100 words.

   (*i*) What differences were given by Chittappan and Kunjamma about greenery, rain etc. between Abu Dhabi and Kerala.

Think, Find and Write

8. Make a comparison between Kerala and Abu Dhabi regarding the points given in Column A of the table given below.

Column A	Kerala	Abu Dhabi
Landform		
Climate		
Currency		
Language spoken		
Clothes usually worn		
Types of buildings		
Traffic on roads		

9. Try to find out the names of the people shown in the currency notes shown in Q 4 and write them below, mentioning the name of the country.

Chapter 25

Spicy Riddles

1. Select the best option.

(i) _____________ is small, skinny and black or brown in colour.

   (a) Cuminseed (*Zeera*) ☐   (b) Garam masala ☐

   (c) Red chilli ☐   (d) None of these ☐

(ii) Aniseed (*Saunf*)

   (a) has a strong smell. ☐   (b) is usually added to food as a powder. ☐

   (c) refreshes the mouth. ☐   (d) All of these. ☐

(iii) In Kuttan's garden _____________ grow.

   (a) cuminseeds ☐   (b) small and big cardamoms ☐

   (c) red chillies ☐   (d) coriander leaves ☐

(iv) _____________ is used to make potato *chaat*.

   (a) Salt ☐   (b) Red chilli powder ☐

   (c) Mango powder (*Amchur*) ☐   (d) All of these ☐

(v) To make potato *chaat* more delicious, we can add

   (a) coriander leaves ☐   (b) cuminseeds (*zeera*) ☐

   (c) black salt ☐   (d) All of these ☐

2. Write 'T' for True and 'F' for False statements.

(i) Red chillies really make the food hot and spicy. ☐

(ii) Turmeric (*Haldi*) makes the food look yellow. ☐

(iii) Cuminseed (*Zeera*) is added to both sweet and salty dishes. ☐

(iv) If Aniseed (*Saunf*) is too much in the food, it makes your eyes and nose water. ☐

(v) Clove (*Laung*) looks like a nail, but actually it is a bud. ☐

3. Fill in the blanks.

    (i) Turmeric (*Haldi*) is loved by everybody because it ______________ both small and big wounds when applied quickly.

    (ii) ______________ makes our stomach healthy.

    (iii) ______________ is chocolate coloured and smells strongly .

    (iv) For making potato *chaat*, boiled potatoes are ______________ before being cut into small pieces.

    (v) ______________ are sprinkled on top of the *chaat* finally.

4. Match the pictures in Column A with their names (spices) in Column B by drawing lines.

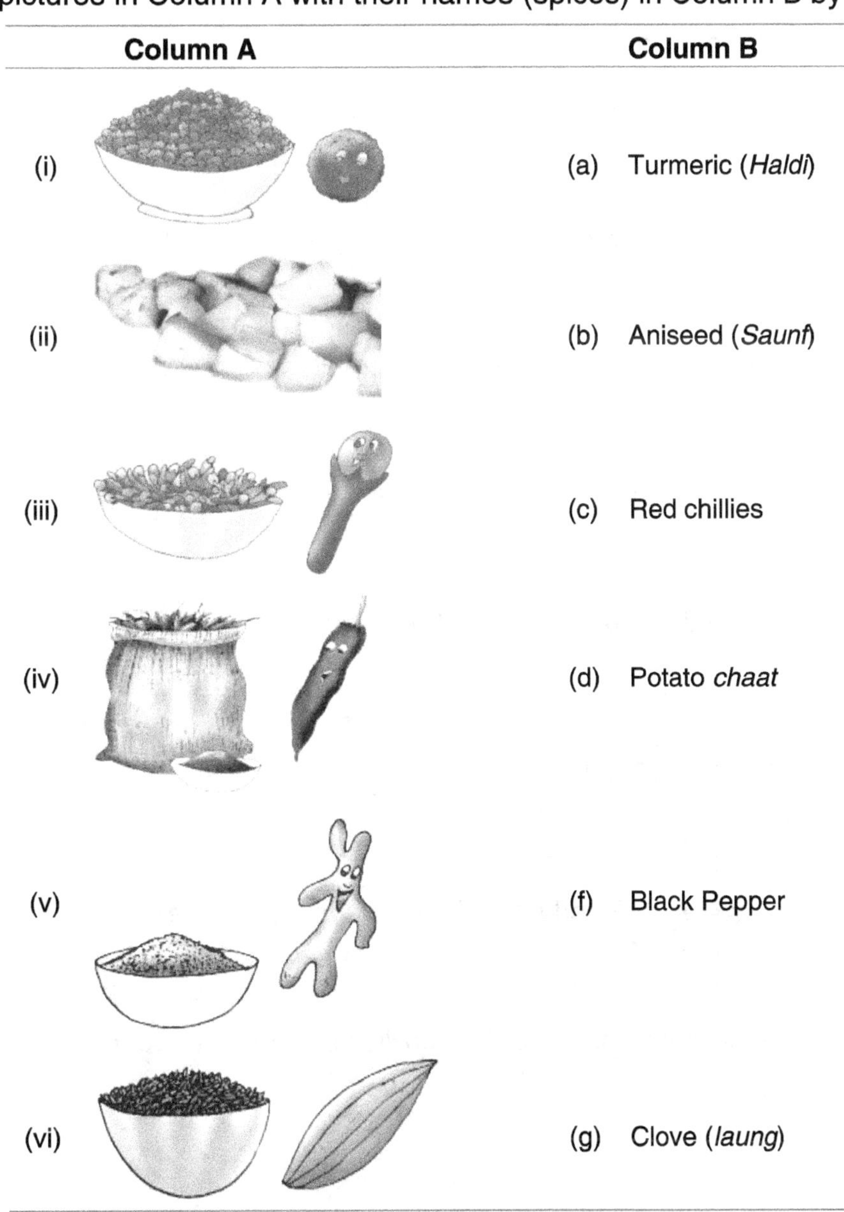

Column A	Column B
(i)	(a) Turmeric (*Haldi*)
(ii)	(b) Aniseed (*Saunf*)
(iii)	(c) Red chillies
(iv)	(d) Potato *chaat*
(v)	(f) Black Pepper
(vi)	(g) Clove (*laung*)

5. Fill in the blanks using the correct options from those given in brackets.

(i) _____________ (Black pepper / Cardamom) is small and round when whole.

(ii) _____________ (Turmeric / Aniseed) heals wounds also.

(iii) _____________ (Clove / Cuminseed) is helpful for toothache.

(iv) _____________ (Red chillies / Pepper) make you gasp "shhee ... shhee ....".

(v) _____________ (Cuminseed / Aniseed) spreads fragrance when roasted.

Very Short Answer Type Question

6. Answer in one word or one sentence.

(i) Which spice makes us cry if we take too much of it?

(ii) Which spice, when added to curd or *jaljeera*, makes them tasty?

(iii) Why is Aniseed (*Saunf)* always eaten after meals?

(iv) Which spice has a strong smell and has the colour of chocolates.

(v) Which spice is used in food to make it taste sour?

Short Answer Type Question

7. Answer in 30 – 40 words.

(i) Differentiate between Aniseed (Saunf) and Cuminseed (Zeera).

(ii) What are the differences between Red chillies and Black pepper?

Long Answer Type Question

8. Answer in 80 – 100 words.

List the items used in potato *chaat* mentioned in the chapter.

Think, Find and Write

9. *Garam masala* is made by grinding many spices together. Write the names of these spices.

10. Write the names of three dishes cooked in your home (one should be a type of *dal*, one a dry vegetable and one a vegetable with gravy), listing the spices and other items used in each. Fill in this information in the table given below. (Take help from your elders)

Type of Dish	Name of dish	Spices used	Other items used
Dal			
Dry vegetable			
Gravy vegetable			

11. Answer in 30 – 40 words.

   (i) In Kuttan's garden, *tejpatta* as well as small and big cardamoms are grown. Write the dishes or beverages in which these spices are used.

12. Names of some spices are given below in jumbled form (some are Indian names). Write the correct names of the spices against each.

   (i) AAGMR AAMALS

   (ii) RACUHM

   (iii) EAZRE

   (iv) DRE ICLILH

   (v) ATAJTPET

Chapter 26

Defence Officer : Wahida

1. Select the best option.

  (i) While in school, Wahida

    (a) climbed mountains. ☐   (b) attended camps. ☐

    (c) was a girl guide. ☐   (d) All of these. ☐

  (ii) Wahida always wanted to become

    (a) a doctor. ☐   (b) someone special. ☐

    (c) a teacher. ☐   (d) a policewoman. ☐

  (iii) Wahida's family thought that a job ___________ would be best for her.

    (a) as a doctor ☐   (b) as a prism ☐

    (c) in the Defence Forces ☐   (d) None of these ☐

  (iv) One of the duties of the medical officer on a ship is to

    (a) provide first aid. ☐   (b) keep all ready for any medical emergency. ☐

    (c) carry out medical check-ups. ☐   (d) All of these. ☐

  (v) To remember all the thirty-six commands to be given in a parade, Wahida practised for

    (a) one month. ☐   (b) a long time. ☐

    (c) a few days. ☐   (d) None of these. ☐

2. Write 'T' for True and 'F' for False statements.

  (i) One of Wahida's sisters works in the Police. ☐

  (ii) Wahida was the first woman who sailed on a naval ship. ☐

  (iii) One of Wahida's duties on the ship is to ensure that no garbage is thrown into the sea. ☐

  (iv) Wahida was not nervous while leading the parade. ☐

  (v) Wahida's father started calling her by the name 'Prism' from her childhood. ☐

3. Fill in the blanks.

(i) Wahida Prism is a Lieutenant Commander in the ___________ .

(ii) Wahida took ___________ training after her MBBS to join the Armed Forces.

(iii) ___________ commands have to be given in a passing out parade.

(iv) She was asked to lead the ___________ after her performance was seen for three years.

(v) She conducts ___________ of all the officers and sailors on board the ship so that they remain healthy.

4. Match the pictures in Column A with their descriptions (Activities) in Column B by drawing lines.

Column A	Column B
(i) 	(a) Wahida in naval uniform
(ii) 	(b) Leading the parade
(iii) 	(c) Giving a command to the troops
(iv) 	(d) At the party after the parade
(v) 	(e) Requesting the Chief Guest to inspect the troops

5. Fill in the blanks using the correct options from those given in brackets.

    (i) Wahida completed her class twelve from ______________ (Jammu /Rajouri).

    (ii) Wahida got her MBBS degree from ______________ (Jammu / Srinagar) Medical College.

    (iii) Wahida's main duty on board the ship is to ensure that all people should remain ______________ (sick / healthy).

    (iv) For joining the Armed Forces, Wahida had to appear for ______________ (a test / an interview).

    (v) When an opportunity was given for going on ______________ (ship / boat), Wahida gave her name.

Very Short Answer Type Question

6. Answer in one word or one sentence.

    (i) Wahida Prism belongs to which place?

    (ii) In what new things Wahida was interested in her childhood?

    (iii) What did Wahida's father want his daughters to become?

    (iv) What made Wahida think of joining the Armed Forces?

    (v) What honour was given to her at the end of her training?

Short Answer Type Question

7. Answer in 30 – 40 words.

    (i) Why did Wahida's parents have to leave their village?

    (ii) What does Wahida tell us about her big dream?

(iii) Why does Wahida want to go in a submarine?

Long Answer Type Question

8. Answer in 80 – 100 words.

(i) What duties does Wahida carry out when she is on board a ship on the sea?

(ii) Describe all the steps Wahida took and the preparations she made for joining the Defence Forces.

Think, Find and Write

9. Find out and write names of five occupations of people working in the Indian Navy besides doctors.

(i)

(ii)

(iii)

(iv)

(v)

Chapter 27

Chuskit Goes to School

1. Select the best option.

(i) Today is a special day for Chuskit because

(a) she is going to school.

(b) it is her birthday.

(c) her father is carrying her to school.

(d) All of these.

(ii) Chuskit's school lies across the

(a) road.

(b) lake.

(c) river.

(d) hill.

(iii) Chuskit was different from other children because

(a) she was blind.

(b) she was deaf.

(c) she did not have one hand.

(d) she could not use her legs.

(iv) Who agreed with Abdul's thinking about how to get Chuskit to school?

(a) The children

(b) The Headmaster and teachers

(c) Chuskit's father

(d) None of these

(v) When Chuskit saw other children laughing and playing on their way to school, she wished

(a) them 'good morning'.

(b) she could go to school with them.

(c) she could play with them.

(d) None of these.

2. Write 'T' for True and 'F' for False statements.

  (i) Chuskit had a good sleep the night before she was to go to school for the first time. ☐

  (ii) When Chuskit wanted to go out of her house, she would tell her mother to put her in the wheelchair. ☐

  (iii) Abdul came to Chuskit's house to play with her. ☐

  (iv) Chuskit's mother told her not to dream of going to school. ☐

  (v) Chuskit was the happiest of all the children when the road to school and the bridge were completed. ☐

3. Match the pictures in Column A with their descriptions in Column B by drawing lines.

Column A	**Column B**
(i) 	(a) Chuskit looking out of her window
(ii) 	(b) Aaba-le carrying Chuskit
(iii) 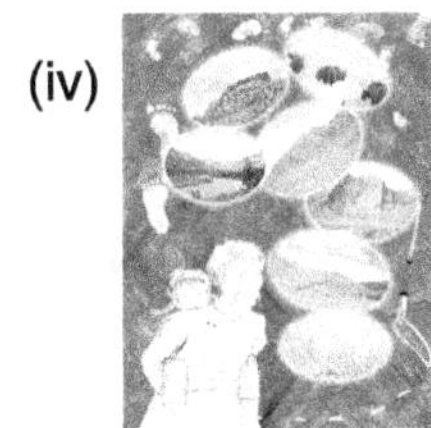	(c) Abdul pushing Chuskit to attend school
(iv) 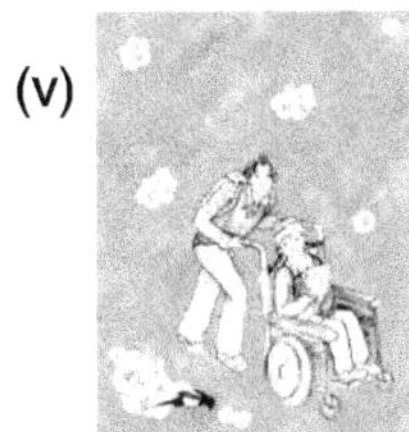	(d) Chuskit watching bus on the road
(v)	(e) Children levelling the road to school

4. Fill in the blanks.

(i) Chuskit has been waiting for this day since long because today she is going to ______________ for the first time.

(ii) Chuskit could not go to school in her wheelchair because the road to school was not ______________ and there was a ______________ to cross.

(iii) Chuskit wanted to ______________ because she wanted to study and play with the other children.

(iv) Everyone got together to work so that ______________ could reach school.

(v) ______________ took help from teacher to make a small bridge across the river.

Very Short Answer Type Question

5. Answer in one word or one sentence.

(i) How old is Chuskit?

(ii) What did Chuskit used to do all day?

(iii) When did Chuskit realise that she did not need her father to carry her everywhere?

(iv) What did Chuskit's grandfather say about not being possible?

Short Answer Type Question

6. Answer in 30 – 40 words.

(i) What explanation did Chuskit give when Abdul asked her the reason of not going to school?

(ii) Describe the way to reach school from Chuskit's house.

(iii) Write Abdul's idea of getting Chuskit to school.

(iv) What was Chuskit's dream? How did it come true?

Long Answer Type Question

8. Answer in 80-100 words.

Who all helped Chuskited to reach the school easily?

Think, Find and Write

9. What is a ramp? Find out and write why is it required in a school where a disabled child like Chuskit has to attend classes.

10. Differently abled persons (also called 'disabled') like Chuskit face many other difficulties in school even after reaching there. Find out and write three such difficulties.

11. Imagine that Chuskit grew up without ever going to school. What difficulties would she face in future? Find out and write any three such difficulties.

Answers

Chapter 1   Going to School

1. (i) (b)   (ii) (d)   (iii) (d)   (iv) (a)   (v) (c)

2. (i) T   (ii) T   (iii) F   (iv) F   (v) F

3. (i) Kerala   (ii) bamboo   (iii) rocky paths   (iv) camel-cart   (v) Sunlight

4. (i) – (b)   (ii) – (d)   (iii) – (a)   (iv) – (c)

Chapter 2   Ear to Ear

1. (i) (b)   (ii) (a)   (iii) (c)   (iv) (b)   (v) (c)

2. (i) F   (ii) T   (iii) T   (iv) F   (v) F

3. (i) feathers   (ii) patterns   (iii) tiny holes   (iv) visible/outer   (v) no hair

4. (i) – (d)   (ii) – (c)   (iii) – (b)   (iv) – (a)

5. (i) Rabbit-Yes   (ii) Parrot-No   (iii) Frog-No   (iv) Deer-Yes   (v) Crocodile-No

Chapter 3   A Day with Nandu

1. (i) (d)   (ii) (c)   (iii) (a)   (iv) (b)   (v) (d)

2. (i) T   (ii) F   (iii) F   (iv) F   (v) T

3. (i) 14 – 15 years old   (ii) the legs and trunks
(iii) the open jungle   (iv) bears, monkeys   (v) tails

4. (i) – (c)   (ii) – (a)   (iii) – (d)   (iv) – (b)

5. (i) – (c)   (ii) – (d)   (iii) – (b)   (iv) – (a)

12. (i) (d),   (ii) (g),   (iii) (a),   (iv) (b),   (v) (f),   (vi) (c),   (vii) (e)

Chapter 4   The Story of Amrita

1. (i) (d)   (ii) (c)   (iii) (a)   (iv) (c)   (v) (b)

2. (i) T   (ii) T   (iii) T   (iv) F   (v) T   (vi) T

3. (i) plants and animals   (ii) trees and animals   (iii) roam freely
(iv) strength   (v) grass   (vi) Jodhpur

4. (i) Picture 3   (ii) Picture 4   (iii) Picture 5   (iv) Picture 1   (v) Picture 2

Chapter 5   Anita and the Honeybees

1. (i) (b)   (ii) (d)   (iii) (d)   (iv) (c)   (v) (a)

2. (i) F   (ii) F   (iii) T   (iv) F   (v) T

3. (i) bee keeping   (ii) October, December   (iii) Queen Bee   (iv) box
(v) one   (vi) Sugar, medicines

4. (i) – (d)   (ii) – (e)   (iii) – (a)   (iv) – (b)   (v) – (c)

5. (i) 8   (ii) 3   (iii) 7   (iv) 5   (v) 6   (vi) 1   (vii) 4   (viii) 2

Chapter 6   Omana's Journey

1. (i) (c)   (ii) (d)   (iii) (c)   (iv) (b)   (v) (d)

2. (i) F   (ii) T   (iii) F   (iv) T   (v) F

3. (i) Omana, Radha   (ii) her bicycle, right   (iii) Two college students
(iv) orange, setting   (v) grandmother's

4. (i) 3   (ii) 6   (iii) 4   (iv) 7   (v) 1   (vi) 8   (vii) 2   (viii) 5

6. (i) – (b)   (ii) – (c)   (iii) – (a)

Chapter 7   From the Window

1. (i) (d)   (ii) (d)   (iii) (a)   (iv) (d)   (v) (c)
2. (i) T   (ii) T   (iii) F   (iv) T   (v) F
3. (i) under, crossing   (ii) river, bridge   (iii) bridges, tunnels
   (iv) two   (v) climbed, upper, read
4. (i) – (e)   (ii) – (c)   (iii) – (a)   (iv) – (d)   (v) – (b)
5. (i) – (c)   (ii) – (d)   (iii) – (b)   (iv) – (a)
10. (i) Cycle   (ii) Bullock Cart
    (iii) Scooter   (iv) Motorcycle
    (v) Truck

Chapter 8   Reaching Grandmother's House

1. (i) (b)   (ii) (d)   (iii) (d)   (iv) (c)   (v) (c)
2. (i) F   (ii) T   (iii) F   (iv) F   (v) F
3. (i) evening   (ii) Appa   (iii) rippling   (iv) *Valiyamma's* (v) long
4. (i) 5   (ii) 8   (iii) 2   (iv) 3   (v) 7   (vi) 1   (vii) 6
   (viii) 4
5. (i) – (c)   (ii) – (d)   (iii) – (b)   (iv) – (a)

Chapter 9   Changing Families

1. (i) (a)   (ii) (c)   (iii) (b)   (iv) (c)   (v) (d)
2. (i) T   (ii) F   (iii) F   (iv) T   (v) T
3. (i) – (d)   (ii) – (f)   (iii) – (e)   (iv) – (b)   (v) – (a)   (vi) – (c)
4.

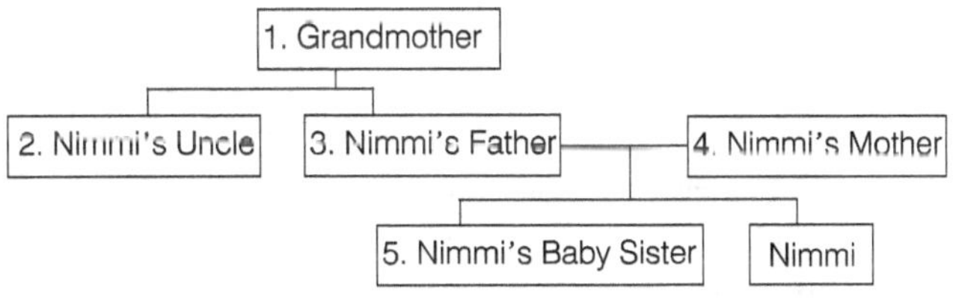

Chapter 10   Hu Tu Tu, Hu Tu Tu

1. (i) (b)   (ii) (d)   (iii) (a)   (iv) (c)   (v) (c)
2. (i) F   (ii) T   (iii) T   (iv) F   (v) F
3. (i) Leela   (ii) Karnam Malleshwari's   (iii) Shyamala   (iv) Rosy   (v) Heera

Chapter 11   The Valley of Flowers

1. (i) (d)   (ii) (a)   (iii) (b)   (iv) (c)   (v) (b)
2. (i) F   (ii) F   (iii) T   (iv) F   (v) T
3. (i) trees, bushes, creepers, water plants
   (ii) day, night
   (iii) banana
   (iv) flowers
   (v) floral
   (vi) Kannauj

Chapter 12   Changing Times

1. (i) (a) (ii) (c) (iii) (b) (iv) (a) (v) (d)

2. (i) T (ii) F (iii) T (iv) F (v) F

3. (i) *neem* and *keekar* trees (ii) unbaked bricks, the house

 (iii) pipes in the toilet (iv) big tents

 (v) cow dung and mud, insects

4. (i) – (d) (ii) – (f) (iii) – (b) (iv) – (e) (v) – (a) (vi) – (c)

Chapter 13   A River's Tale

1. (i) (b) (ii) (a) (iii) (c) (iv) (d) (v) (c)

2. (i) F (ii) F (iii) T (iv) F (v) T

3. (i) polluted (ii) yellow (iii) does not dissolve (iv) kill (v) clean

4. (i) DISSOLVE (ii) SHERBET (iii) MUSTARD OIL (iv) COOKING (v) UTENSILS (vi) FACTORIES

 (vii) BATHING (viii) WASHING (ix) FLOWING (x) DRINKING

5. (i) – (d) (ii) – (e) (iii) – (a) (iv) – (b) (v) – (c)

Chapter 14   Basva's Farm

1. (i) (b) (ii) (b) (iii) (d) (iv) (c) (v) (c)

2. (i) F (ii) T (iii) F (iv) F (v) T

3. (i) *Khunti* - (c) (ii) *illige* - (a) (iii) *Kurige* - (b)

4. (i) – (e) (ii) – (c) (iii) – (f) (iv) – (a) (v) – (b) (vi) – (d)

5. (i) onion seeds (ii) *khunti* (iii) Belvanika, Karnataka

 (iv) the right amount, regular (v) Weeds

Chapter 15   From Market to Home

1. (i) (b) (ii) (c) (iii) (c) (iv) (a) (v) (d)

2. (i) T (ii) T (iii) F (iv) F (v) F

3. (i) 7:30 AM (ii) gunny bags and baskets (iii) mandi

 (iv) regular customers (v) 10 PM

4. (i) – (c) (ii) – (a) (iii) – (d) (iv) – (b)

5. (i) – (d) (ii) – (a) (iii) – (e) (iv) – (b) (v) – (c) (vi) – (f)

Chapter 16   A Busy Month

1. (i) (d) (ii) (a) (iii) (d) (iv) (c) (v) (b)

2. (i) F (ii) T (iii) T (iv) F (v) T

3. (i) food (ii) male (iii) sharp (iv) sides, chew (v) breaking and crushing

4. (i) – (e) (ii) – (f) (iii) – (a) (iv) – (b) (v) – (d) (vi) – (c)

5. 1–Weaver bird 2–Tailor bird 3–Barbet 4–Sunbird 5–*Koel* 6–Crow 7–Dove 8–Indian Robin

Chapter 17   Nandita in Mumbai

1. (i) (c) (ii) (d) (iii) (a) (iv) (b) (v) (c)

2. (i) F (ii) F (iii) T (iv) F (v) F

3. (i) – (f) (ii) – (e) (iii) – (b) (iv) – (c) (v) – (d) (vi) – (a)

4. (i) *Mama's* street (ii) Nandita's *Mami* (iii) *Chowpatti*

 (iv) Nandita's *Mama* (v) in the hospital

Chapter 18   Too Much Water, Too Little Water

1. (i) (b)   (ii) (a)   (iii) (c)   (iv) (c)   (v) (d)
2. (i) T   (ii) F   (iii) T   (iv) F   (v) F
3. (i) – (c)   (ii) – (a)   (iii) – (e)   (iv) – (b)   (v) – (d)
4. (i) – (c)   (ii) – (d)   (iii) – (a)   (iv) – (b)
5. (i) impure   (ii) slowly   (iii) tears   (iv) water
   (v) very little water   (vi) sugar   (vii) diarrhoea and vomiting   (viii) water fit for drinking

Chapter 19   Abdul in the Garden

1. (i) (b)   (ii) (d)   (iii) (a)   (iv) (c)   (v) (a)
2. (i) F   (ii) F   (iii) T   (iv) T   (v) T
3. (i) Abdul, *Abbu* (ii) support (iii) its roots were longer   (iv) remained firm   (v) they reach water
4. (i) – (e)   (ii) – (c)   (iii) – (b)   (iv) – (f)   (v) – (d)   (vi) – (a)
5. (i) carrot   (ii) rough   (iii) banyan   (iv) desert oak
7. (i) VEGETABLES (ii) DESERT OAK (iii) HANGING ROOTS (iv) RADISH (v) COTTON WOOL

Chapter 20   Eating Together

1. (i) (c)   (ii) (b)   (iii) (c)   (iv) (d)   (v) (a)
2. (i) F   (ii) T   (iii) F   (iv) F   (v) T
3. (i) her uncle's wedding   (ii) every child's   (iii) washing our hands
   (iv) fresh, hot and properly cooked   (v) study properly
4. (i) *pitha*   (ii) *Uruka*   (iii) *kadahi*   (iv) *pat, Muga mekhala-chador*
5. (i) – (c)   (ii) – (a)   (iii) – (d)   (iv) – (b)

Chapter 21   Food and Fun

1. (i) (c)   (ii) (c)   (iii) (b)   (iv) (d)   (v) (a)
2. (i) F   (ii) F   (iii) F   (iv) T   (v) T
3. (i) the Gurudwara   (ii) activity   (iii) the *channa* and *urad dal*
   (iv) *langar*   (v) in the end   (vi) flour   (vii) halwa
4. (i) – (c)   (ii) – (a)   (iii) – (d)   (iv) – (b)

Chapter 22   The World in my Home

1. (i) (a)   (ii) (d)   (iii) (c)   (iv) (b)   (v) (c)
2. (i) F   (ii) T   (iii) T   (iv) T   (v) F
3. (i) – (f)   (ii) – (d)   (iii) – (g)   (iv) – (a)   (v) – (c)   (vi) – (b)   (vii) – (e)
4. (i) TV programmes   (ii) playing   (iii) five *kulfis*
   (iv) grind grain   (v) hopscotch

Chapter 23   Pochampalli

1. (i) (a)   (ii) (c)   (iii) (c)   (iv) (b)   (v) (d)
2. (i) F   (ii) F   (iii) T   (iv) T   (v) T
3. (i) – (c)   (ii) – (e)   (iii) – (a)   (iv) – (b)   (v) – (d)
4. (i) boiling   (ii) drying   (iii) thread   (iv) sarees   (v) cotton
   (vi) bright   (vii) needles
6. (i) THREAD   (ii) TRADITIONAL   (iii) WEAVING
   (iv) BUNDLES   (v) SHOPKEEPERS   (vi) PRECIOUS
   (vii) BOILING WATER   (viii) KULLU SHAWLS   (ix) POCHAMPALLI   (x) MUKHTAPUR

Chapter 24   Home and Abroad

1. (i) (c)　　　(ii) (a)　　　(iii) (c)　　　(iv) (b)　　　(v) (d)
2. (i) F　　　(ii) T　　　(iii) F　　　(iv) T　　　(v) F
3. (i) *Chittappan* and his family　　(ii) *Chittappan*　　(iii) Shanta, Sashi
(iv) Abu Dhabi, Kerala, Chennai and Kochi　　(v) precious
4. (i) – (c)　　　(ii) – (e)　　　(iii) – (b)　　　(iv) – (a)　　　(v) – (d)

Chapter 25   Spicy Riddles

1. (i) (a)　　　(ii) (c)　　　(iii) (b)　　　(iv) (d)　　　(v) (d)
2. (i) T　　　(ii) T　　　(iii) F　　　(iv) F　　　(v) T
3. (i) heals　　(ii) Aniseed (*Saunf*)　　(iii) Clove (*laung*) (iv) peeled
(v) Chopped coriander leaves
4. (i) – (f)　　　(ii) – (d)　　　(iii) – (g)　　　(iv) – (c)　　　(v) – (a)　　　(vi) – (b)
5. (i) Black pepper　(ii) Turmeric　(iii) Clove　　(iv) Red chillies　(v) Cuminseed

Chapter 26   Defence Officer : Wahida

1. (i) (d)　　　(ii) (b)　　　(iii) (c)　　　(iv) (d)　　　(v) (a)
2. (i) T　　　(ii) F　　　(iii) F　　　(iv) T　　　(v) T
3. (i) Indian Navy　(ii) six months (iii) Thirty-six　(iv) passing out parade　(v) medical check-up
4. (i) – (e)　　　(ii) – (d)　　　(iii) – (c)　　　(iv) – (a)　　　(v) – (b)
5. (i) Rajouri　　(ii) Jammu　　(iii) healthy　　(iv) an interview　(v) ship

Chapter 27   Chuskit Goes to School

1. (i) (a)　　　(ii) (c)　　　(iii) (d)　　　(iv) (b)　　　(v) (b)
2. (i) F　　　(ii) T　　　(iii) F　　　(iv) F　　　(v) T
3. (i) – (d)　　　(ii) – (a)　　　(iii) – (e)　　　(iv) – (b)　　　(v) – (c)
4. (i) school　　(ii) level, river　(iii) join the school　　(iv) Chuskit　(v) The older children